Victoria Vivente currently works as a vulnerability specialist in banking. She is an accredited financial counsellor (money crisis specialist) and financial coach (money behaviour specialist) who lives in Sydney (Gadigal Country) and specialises in strategic advocacy – policy that makes banking better for people experiencing vulnerability. Victoria has written for *The West Australian* and has also been featured on Channel 9 and the ABC. In her 'spare time', she is studying to become a lawyer.

Know Your Worth

Victoria Vivente

affirm
press

affirm
press

First published by Affirm Press in 2025
Bunurong/Boon Wurrung Country
28 Thistlethwaite Street
South Melbourne VIC 3205
affirmpress.com.au

10 9 8 7 6 5 4 3 2 1

Affirm Press is located on the unceded land of the Bunurong/Boon Wurrung peoples of
the Kulin Nation. Affirm Press pays respect to their Elders past and present.

 A catalogue record for this
book is available from the
National Library of Australia

ISBN: 9781923022430 (paperback)

Cover design by Alissa Dinallo © Affirm Press
Typeset in 11.25/15.5 pt Adobe Caslon Pro by Post Pre-press Group, Brisbane
Printed and bound in China by C&C Offset Printing Co., Ltd.

 MIX
Paper | Supporting
responsible forestry
FSC® C008047

For Pippin, who didn't care if it was possible.

For Richard, who showed me anything was possible.

For Ben, who kept it possible.

For Kelly, who made it possible.

For Stella and Olive, for whom I want everything to be possible.

And for my clients, whose generosity, vulnerability and humour have allowed them to achieve so much that they believed to be impossible.

Contents

Introduction

Have you ever felt like you don't quite 'get' money like everyone else? Do you struggle to understand what people are even talking about, let alone put whole personal money systems into practice? It's more common than you think. Every day, when I worked as a financial counsellor and financial coach, clients would come into my office, positive they were the only ones struggling with their money. 'It's fair to say that people are more likely to talk about their sex lives or religion than they are to talk about money,' says Fiona Guthrie, former Chief Executive of Financial Counselling Australia. She's right. Most people are pretending they know what they're doing when it comes to money, and no one is talking about it when they aren't.

The reality is that 'knowing about money' is not simple because our relationship with money operates within a clusterfuck of other things. Here's what it looks like:

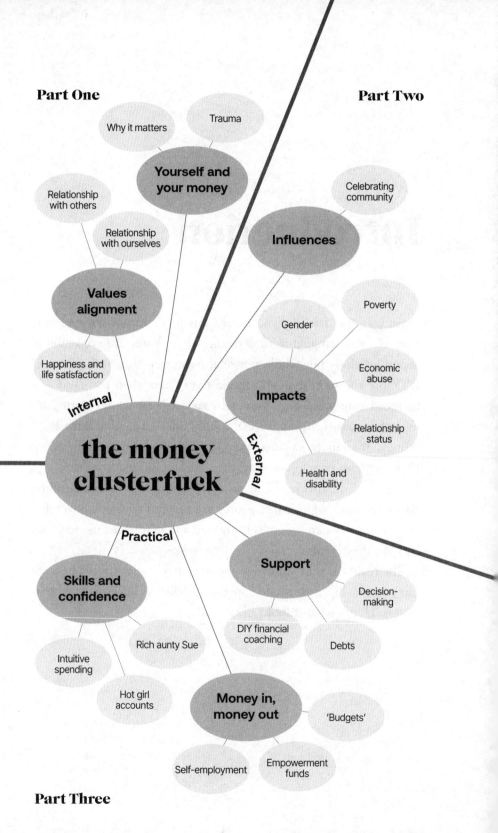

Part One

Part Two

Trauma

Yourself and your money

Why it matters

Relationship with others

Relationship with ourselves

Values alignment

Happiness and life satisfaction

Celebrating community

Influences

Poverty

Gender

Economic abuse

Impacts

Relationship status

Health and disability

Internal

External

the money clusterfuck

Practical

Skills and confidence

Intuitive spending

Rich aunty Sue

Hot girl accounts

Support

Decision-making

DIY financial coaching

Debts

Money in, money out

'Budgets'

Self-employment

Empowerment funds

Part Three

Some money books will tell you to stop spending and run your life with a spreadsheet, where every dollar is accounted for, but not this one. *Know Your Worth* is about teasing apart the clusterfuck, understanding all the elements and creating personalised, easy choices for you to build a great relationship with your money.

This book is broken up into three parts: Part 1 looks at internal factors that influence our money; in Part 2, we talk about the external factors that influence our money; and in Part 3 we dive into practical tools and support to improve our money skills and confidence.

By the time you get to the end of this book, not only will you have a thorough understanding of the money basics, but you'll also know how your personal experiences have shaped your relationship with money and money habits. You'll come out of *Know Your Worth* with a fully customised plan to nail your money in the way that works best for you.

This book is for you if:

- you've been wondering how everyone seems to have their shit together except for you
- you feel like you're falling behind where you think you 'should be'
- spending money is one of your favourite ways to feel better, even when it doesn't really make you feel better
- you feel like you have no idea about money, how to keep it or how to manage it
- you hate talking about money and sometimes get a prickly sense of shame when you think about it
- you've never picked up a money book in your life
- you've picked up a money book, flicked through it and thought, 'Okay, that is absolutely not for me'
- you've worked your way through a money book, implemented a couple of steps and then got confused or fell off the wagon.

While this book is about all things money, it's about so much more – because there really is more to our money than just 'money'.

What you can expect to find in these pages:

- your sudden qualification as a train driver
- why there's tofu at the hunting club
- cake
- tasselled handbaskets with snacks
- jars of rocks
- vitamin E cream
- why dieting is a load of shit
- witches, cauldrons and Gandalf
- period talk
- Jennifer Coolidge.

I am deadly serious when I tell you all this and more awaits you. It will be the least money-speak money book you've ever read. Guaranteed. There are many finance books that tell you how to make money, grow your money and manage your money within an inch of its life. This book is the prequel to those books. It's about how to know your worth and get your money's worth.

This sounds great, but why should I listen to you?

I'm Victoria, a qualified, accredited financial counsellor based in Australia. I've also worked as a financial coach, which is slightly different. I now work in customer advocacy in the banking industry. If those words mean absolutely nothing, that's okay. There are a lot of 'financy' jobs out there, so I'll go through them now to make sure we're on the same page.

Financial counselling

In Australia, financial counselling is a free, government-funded and industry-funded service to help people in financial crisis or difficulty. This means financial counsellors help people without having to charge them. They work independently and always fight for the client.

When I was a financial counsellor, I worked with young people who had tens (or hundreds) of thousands of dollars of debt. I had clients whose homes we couldn't save from repossession. I had clients who experienced a life-changing injury and were able to claim on their superannuation insurance. I've helped people file for bankruptcy and get legal assistance to apply for probate after their partner died. I've helped negotiate legal fees, I've negotiated reduced financial settlements for debts, I've begged banks to waive debts. I've sat listening to hold music for three hours (and talked with my mouth full when they finally answered). Once, I told a bank I was invoicing them for my botox because their antics were ageing me.

But there were two core things I saw in every person who walked through my door:

1. They all had money strengths.
2. They all had a voice, no matter how small, that said, 'I'm not ready to give up yet.'

So, if you're reading this book, there's a pretty high chance you have money strengths. If all of my clients did, despite being in financial crisis, I'm confident you do, too.

Financial coaching

Unlike financial counsellors, financial coaches don't (currently) need to be registered or have a formal qualification, though there are some (non-Australian tertiary-accredited) courses around. Despite this, a good financial coach is still an incredible person to have in your corner.

While a financial counsellor's job is to fix a problem that is usually urgent, a financial coach helps people understand their strengths, triggers and behaviours, and develop financial resilience and confidence. A lot of financial coaching is about unpacking money lessons or attitudes picked up over time.

When I was a financial coach, I worked with a lot of people on high incomes who had never been taught how to manage money and were still living pay cheque to pay cheque. I worked with people who had left, were leaving or were planning to leave relationships. I worked with people who had been victimised by romance scams, who couldn't stop money from slipping through their fingers (even though they weren't in debt) and who were put off from taking financial steps for lots of different reasons. Once people started to think about money without judgement, their life goals totally changed. I'm not being dramatic when I say financial coaching can be life-changing.

Banking and customer advocacy

Each bank in Australia has a Customer Advocate. The Customer Advocate's job is to make sure the bank is treating its customers fairly – with its products, procedures, policies, interactions, outcomes and community work. Each bank does it slightly differently, and while a Customer Advocate doesn't review complaints at the request of a customer, they have the right to examine any customer matter or issue they decide is needed. I currently work in the best Customer Advocate team in Australia (totally unbiased review by me).

Some Customer Advocate teams support customer-facing staff with situations that need guidance and support: a customer might be experiencing elder financial abuse through their power of attorney, they might be the victim of a scam, or there might be unusual activity on their account that deserves further investigation. Alternatively, a staff member might have concerns about a customer's capacity to make financial decisions.

The team may also work on policy, procedure, skills and training to make sure customers are being treated fairly, especially if they're experiencing vulnerability. I'm sure we all have a story of when a bank let us, or someone we know, down. Customer Advocates and their teams work in banks to try to prevent that from happening, and to make it right when it does.

Everything else

I have a financial literacy Instagram account, @bad.bitch.money, where I talk about non-judgemental ways to know your worth and get your money's worth. It stemmed from my young financial counselling clients who wanted to know more about money without being preached to.

I also have a fortnightly newsletter, 'Shambolic: newsletter of chaos'. This is where I do a deeper dive into money stuff (and sometimes life stuff). A couple of those newsletters have made their way into this book.

I've been very lucky to have clients, customers and other financial counsellors and coaches share their stories with me. I know how much 'money stuff' affects 'life stuff' and vice versa. Everyone has seen some shit and everyone has done some shit. This book is built on the experiences of people who have all done that shit (or are still doing it!).

A note on curiosity

Diving into money work or self-work (or life in general, actually) can bring up a lot of negative emotions. We might be afraid, disappointed, blaming, judgemental. That's pretty normal. Rather than trying to treat ourselves with kindness and compassion, let's aim for curiosity. The current emotional and/or financial place you're in hasn't happened overnight, and working through it will take time and a desire to understand what drives you. (Of course, kindness and compassion are the ultimate goals – but sometimes that's a bit much for us to ask of ourselves, and they don't always help us put new plans in place.)

A note on compassion versus accountability

You might work your way through this book and think there's a lot of justifying and not a lot of accountability. That's because years of client work, both in financial counselling and financial coaching, have taught me that most people don't need accountability. They need help seeing their own strengths, understanding what has impacted their past and current money decisions, and someone who can say 'sounds like you did your best at the time'. Financial counselling is all about providing choices, not directions. This book does the same.

Judging a person for not getting it right, not hitting their goal or going backwards is not only unhelpful, but harmful. People carry that judgement for a long time, whether that comes from a family member, friend or professional. It's the difference between blaming a plant for not growing where it's planted and helping a plant find the right soil, fertiliser and sun-to-water ratio to help it grow where it's planted.

There are questions at the end of each chapter to spark conversations with yourself and others, and I've also included step-by-step processes for putting work into practice. You can create your own accountabilities out of these chapters if you like. But you also might find some parts overwhelming or completely misaligned with your personality. You haven't failed the book or yourself if you don't follow everything in it.

If this happens, use your discretion, gut instinct and any other mechanism to manipulate or soften these strategies. Skip them totally or circle back to them on a high-energy day. There's no wrong way to be on this journey. All I ask of you is to commit to it.

Agreement between 'now me' and 'future me'

I am prepared to try, even if I must try again (and again and again). If I can't do it in a straight line, I will curve and dance and sometimes stumble when my feet hurt. I will do it loudly, or quietly, or sometimes one or the other, or both, knowing the floodlight and the candle are not competing for the same glow. I will be patient if I sometimes feel I am doing it badly, remembering that I didn't get where I am overnight. Even if I don't trust the journey yet, I can trust myself to start walking down the path to see where it leads.

Part 1

Internal factors that influence our money

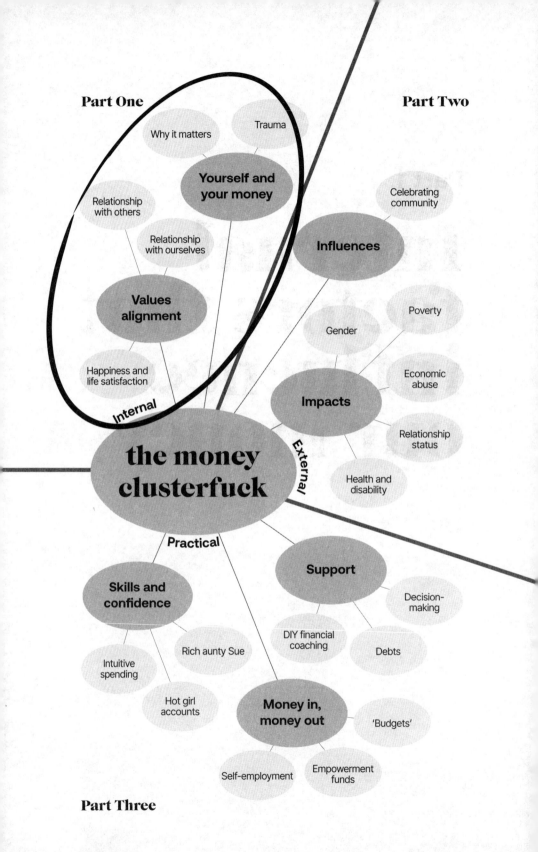

Part One

Why it matters

Trauma

Yourself and your money

Relationship with others

Relationship with ourselves

Values alignment

Happiness and life satisfaction

Internal

Part Two

Celebrating community

Influences

Gender

Poverty

Economic abuse

Impacts

Relationship status

Health and disability

External

the money clusterfuck

Practical

Support

Decision-making

DIY financial coaching

Debts

Skills and confidence

Rich aunty Sue

Intuitive spending

Hot girl accounts

Money in, money out

'Budgets'

Self-employment

Empowerment funds

Part Three

Part 1 focuses on the clusterfuck that forms our values alignment. We'll do a deep dive into resisting the timeline – and whether the Great Australian Dream is actually your great Australian nightmare. We'll talk about Elton John, Madonna, curiosity, train wrecks and how much your life matters and how much it doesn't. It features cake, a diorama and a (now vintage) map of the Perth train system.

We'll talk about being tofu at a hunting party and how dating yourself as an adult is bloody scary but also bloody worth it. We'll talk about finding happiness when the world is going to hell in a handbasket, and how making sure we take time to find our happiness enables us to be better global citizens.

We'll talk about how to start pulling apart what is actually important to you versus what you think people around you need to see. We're going to talk about how to treat yourself as the love of your life, and how just because some friendships end (even the long ones), they aren't failures.

All these things impact our money – the way we save it, the way we spend it and the way we treat it. All the budgeting advice in the world is going to last as long as ice cream out of the freezer unless we are curious about ourselves and how we support or sabotage our own money habits.

Chapter 1

Fuck the timeline

When I started drafting notes for this book, there was a week in which the following was posted on my Instagram feed:

- two pregnancies
- a wedding
- three engagements
- a new house.

Nothing says you've hit your 30s like that kind of week on the feed.

It was around this time when I started having the 'oh god, is this it?' crisis (not for the first time). Is this what my next 35 years will look like? I had a good job, great friends, fun hobbies. The thought that I would work, buy a house, get married and have kids left me absolutely terrified. I started looking for alternatives, but there weren't many people publicly breaking away from the house-baby-wedding or career-baby-house journey.

Generally, no one is sharing the lowlights or when they drift off 'the path'. What does this do for the rest of us? It creates a diorama of the ideal life. Great job, loving partner, a home you own (a home being preferred to an apartment, of course), probably kids. And if it's too early for that to be your diorama, it's usually stacks of travel, Gucci bags and glorious bottomless brunches without wearing the same outfit twice.

The happiness diorama

I'm just a girl, standing in front of a diorama, thinking, 'Cute, but not for me.' I've done it both ways. I've followed the script – had a house, loving partner, long-term plans – and then I got a few years in and was like, 'Whoa, doing this feels very bad for me.' So I got out, with lots of hurt and chaos in the process, and then proceeded to stagnate in a basic admin job for almost five years. It took me years to find my way to a new path.

I've had friends who have done the opposite – been long-term happily single, and then met someone and ended up with a diorama very similar to the above. Some people do the diorama twice, or three times. There's nothing wrong with a life that looks like this diorama – as long as you've chosen that life and it fills you with peace and joy. As we go through Part 1, remember:

1. Your timeline does not have to look like anyone else's. It doesn't even need the same milestone markers.
2. You are not too late, or too early. There is time to start and time to change your mind.

Think of your personal timeline as a train. We'll be talking about the passengers, the stations behind us, the stations ahead, railway maintenance and how to manage the costs of keeping that train on its tracks. Did I lose you halfway through the metaphor? That's okay, we've got plenty of time to work it out.

Even when the trains are the same, the journeys are different. Here is a train map for Perth, Australia, where I grew up (it's slightly out of date, but I chose it for its fabulous clarity):

On a surface level, Perth trains are roughly the same; they all carry passengers, have distinct upholstery on the seats and have an overcrowding problem during peak hour. And, of course, they all start in Perth. But from there, you choose a direction, how far you go, and the time you get on the train. Are you taking your train to the end of the line, or getting off a few stops in? Are you battling other people for seats in peak hour, or coming to the station after everyone's gone to work?

When it comes to Perth passenger trains, there are three different types, and this fits most people, too. You can be career-focused, family-focused or hobby-focused. When you fit one of these types, it can still feel like everyone else is doing it better than you.

Even when you're surrounded by people on the same path as you, there are still differences that make you tilt your head and think, 'Am I doing this right? Is this how it's supposed to work?'

And what do you do when you feel like none of those types really fit? Are you even a passenger train at all? Perhaps you're a cargo train with a single goal, or a luxury train cruising through the countryside?

Thinking of ourselves as driving a train allows us to continually affirm that our path is allowed to be different. We have each been on a different train, with different stations, different passengers and different destinations in mind. Or if you don't know what your destination is yet (or ever), you've seen other people's destinations and know there's no way in hell you're heading to the same place.

Despite this, it's hard not to compare your route to someone else's. It's easy to just say 'don't worry about other people and what they're doing', but personally, telling me not to worry about something has never stopped me from worrying about it.

Instead, if we acknowledge that sometimes we get nervous about what other people are doing, and then refocus on our own train, we can hold room for both. After all, the 'ideal' timeline is a made-up thing, and while we can acknowledge that the timelines of people around us make us nervous, jealous or sad, at the end of the day, if you knew everything about a person's timeline, you probably wouldn't swap them for it.

We'll talk more about finding the things and people that help us shape who is on the train and where it's going in Chapters 3, 4 and 5. But for now, focus on noticing your worry, acknowledging it, and remembering your train is running on its own tracks.

You are not too late, or too early

You know what I love the most about passenger trains? You can get off and turn around if you realise you're going in the wrong direction or you've gone too far. There's always time. Time to change your mind, time to chuck it in the bin, time to start fresh, time to make a mess and put your pieces back in different places. There is time to do more, less or even nothing for a while. Sure, life is short. But it's also the longest story we get to write.

I had a friend in high school who was both academically and musically talented. He decided that he didn't want that life – he wanted to dance. So, he started teaching himself when he was 16 and hasn't looked back. Fifteen years later, he's a dancer for Madonna. No word of a lie. He realised he was going in the wrong direction and changed trains – and you can, too.

Case study: Marg, 62

Marg came to financial coaching because she felt she was struggling financially. She had separated from her husband and was finalising the financial settlement and taking over the mortgage, though she had been delaying this process for over a year. While Marg felt like she was struggling financially (she worked four days a week in community services, was studying for a diploma and had two teenage children), she actually had a meticulous budget and savings accounts. What Marg discovered was that her fear of taking over the mortgage and the 'end' of her marriage were the real problems. What was holding her back from finalising the settlement was the (scary) freedom of having to look her own goals in the eye. Marg's secret dream was to travel more, including seeing her family interstate and travelling overseas, which she had never done before.

By the time she finished coaching, she had booked a local trip and a trip to see her family, had submitted the forms for the financial separation, and had applied for her passport.

What would you want out of life if you got to choose and never had to explain yourself to anyone? What would you want to do for work (if anything)? Who would you want for a partner (if anyone)? How would you put yourself out in the world? What would you change, and what would you keep the same?

What if you don't know what you want?

It's pretty hard to focus on your own train when you're still stuck at the station wondering which platform to choose. Sometimes freedom can be overwhelming, and rather than grasping at anything and everything because we're terrified we won't get enough out of life, it can be helpful to take a mindful pause before moving forward. Maybe we'll take a look at the map of train routes and see what destination looks good, or maybe we'll patiently wait for a train we have a good feeling about. Either way, we're letting ourselves and the universe know that we're open to new opportunities.

When I was in my late 20s and working a basic admin job for the fourth year running, I got to the point where I wanted to do something else for work – not even a career, just something else – but I didn't have a clue what I wanted. So, I did two things: when I drove to work every day, I said, out loud, that I was grateful for the job I had, and then I said that I was open to new opportunities.

The gratitude kept me from feeling resentful towards my job or upset about feeling stuck, and being open to new possibilities allowed me to be curious. A few months later, I read something about financial counselling. I'd never heard of it before, but when I googled what it was, I was like, 'Ah, that's what I'm supposed to do next.'

Pausing gives us grace when we're feeling stuck, confused or uninspired about what to do next. And it doesn't have to be about work, either. It can apply to other things, too:

- 'I'm open to opportunities for a new hobby.'
- 'I'm open to opportunities to meet new people.'
- 'I'm open to opportunities to find an incredible partner.'
- 'I'm open to opportunities to find a great travel destination.'
- 'I'm open to opportunities to see life differently.'

If you want something different but aren't sure what to do, 'open to opportunities' gives your brain a nudge to keep your eyes and ears alert, without having to find the full solution first.

A note on work and the work timeline

There seem to be two strong camps on working in the modern age:

- **People who live to work:** These people are hustling and progressing, they're putting in the commitment to get their career where they want it to be. They've got a career or business progression plan. They're shooting for the stars and committed to the biscuit.
- **People who work to live:** These people are working to make money to fund their life outside work. Whether that's travel, rescuing animals, retiring early or raising a family, these people do what is in their job description or business plan; no more, no less. They're at work to make money to live a good life.

Maybe you're struggling to pick a camp and fit better with the smaller group off to the side, the in-betweeners. These people haven't quite found a vibe in either camp yet. Maybe they're not doing either, or maybe they're doing a bit of both. But which camp is the right one?

Luckily, you're driving your train. It's okay if you don't know where your train is headed, so long as you just pick one; you can always turn it around. But it's worthwhile reflecting on the track you chose, or the one you want to shift onto. Did you pick this track because you like the look of the route and destination? Or has outside influence pushed you onto it?

Here are some signs you might need to revisit your work timeline:

- You buy things you don't really need as a reward for making it through the day, or because you're bored.
- You get the Sunday scaries every week.
- You take a lot of sick days, even though you're not sick.
- You're praying for redundancy.
- You leave work feeling miserable, drained and wondering how you ended up selling your soul to the capitalist devil.

It doesn't matter which track you choose, but it does matter that you're content with the hours you spend on it. If not, it might be time for an 'open to opportunities' period. Your life-career balance has a huge impact on your spending, saving and general relationship with money, and there's no time to waste on things you don't like.

Your time is valuable

The average person only has 4000 weeks on Earth. Terrifying. In the cosmic calendar, popularised by Carl Sagan, the entire history of the universe is represented on a single 12-month calendar – and the whole of humanity, starting from the primitive humans of 2.5 million years ago, starts at 10.24pm on 31 December. Our lives make up a hundredth of a millisecond, at most. You don't have much to spare – and, as we all know, anything rare is valuable.

We'll talk about this more in the next chapter, but everyone has the capacity to make positive change, despite being a blip in the universe's history. And by sorting out your money basics, you can clear a heap of headspace so you can make the most out of that tiny blip.

Nuggets
and sauce

(takeaways) from Chapter 1

Remember, people are selective about what they share; don't get stuck looking through the window of a diorama because it looks good from the outside. Consider what *you* actually want.

———————

When thinking about your own train and what your journey might look like, aim for curiosity.

———————

It doesn't matter where we are on the journey; we're still allowed to change direction or start afresh. Are you happy with the direction you're headed?

———————

If we know we want something different, but don't know what, we can leave ourselves 'open to opportunities'. Our time is valuable and limited. Consider if this changes the way you think about a risk or chance you want to take.

Reflective questions

Am I on the diorama path? Do I feel happy or trapped by that?

What lowlights or 'off the beaten path' lives am I aware of that I don't see on social media, and why don't I see them?

How can I check in with myself to make sure I'm being curious instead of critical?

If someone asked me about my train, how would I describe it?

Do I feel safe and happy with the direction my train is going in, or do I feel like I'm going the wrong way or stuck at a station?

Do I feel like I'm running early or late in life? Why?

Are there opportunities I want to be open to?

Am I a career person, a lifestyle person or an in-betweener? Is that what I want?

Do I need to revisit my work timeline?

Am I content with how I'm spending my 4000 weeks?

Chapter 2

Tofu at a hunting party

When I was in my 20s, I went vegan for a few years. It's a long, boring story, but basically, I ate *a lot* of tofu. I ate tofu three times a day for months on end.

Now imagine if I swanned into the Game Hunters Association of Australia and told them they should turn vegan and eat a kilogram of tofu per day. My guess is they would be unlikely to welcome me into their arms. But I'd probably be welcomed into vegan networking groups. Same person, different outcomes. Nothing about me changed, just my surroundings.

Manifestation coach and general icon Kira Matthews talks about this concept and asks how much energy you're prepared to exert to stay in a room you aren't comfortable in. Thankfully, it's not a case of being wrong for the room. It's a case of *finding the right room*.

If you're surrounded by people who love you for who you are and like themselves for who they are, your spending is going to be impacted in a positive way. You'll be able to have honest conversations about your budget, you won't feel the need to spend in certain ways to 'keep up' and you'll feel safe liking different things to your friends. If you're surrounded by people who are passionate about striving and achieving, you'll start to believe good things are possible for you, too.

You are shaped by all the people you choose to spend time with. Don't dull your colours just because you're surrounded by people who see in black and white. Like Goldilocks and her bed, or my search for a tofu-loving audience, you might have to hunt around for people who are 'just right'. And that is okay. It's also okay to grieve leaving people behind as you search, and this applies to your money, too. Spreadsheets might not work, strict mapping might not work, a five-account system might not work. You are not the problem. You just haven't found the right solution for you.

Case study: Billie, 27

Billie came to financial counselling to get help with a credit card debt that had got a bit out of hand. We worked out a plan to cancel the card and pay the remaining balance within 12 months, as well as a couple of other budgeting strategies. When we were talking about the credit card and why she'd had it for so long, Billie talked about her three friends from primary school. She still hung out with them a lot, even though she felt like she didn't quite fit in with them anymore. Her friends all had credit cards and valued lots of long 'dinner and drinks' meals with a lot of surface-level chat.

While Billie loved seeing this group, she was craving something else and wanted to have other activities that brought her joy without spending hundreds of dollars a month. We talked about her childhood hobbies, things she's been interested in, and what it might look like to add them into her life.

At her follow-up appointment a month later, Billie had joined a netball team. This brought her into a different circle, and because of the Saturday games, she couldn't go to as many dinners with the girls. She loved the teamwork and being outside. Billie was considering finding a book club to get involved in some deeper conversations.

She was still paying down the credit card and had hugely reduced the financial pressure of keeping up with her primary school gang, but she didn't feel like she'd lost a single thing in the process.

Keep searching for your people, and keep learning about what you like in others and how they bring out the best parts of yourself. Here are some of the responses I got when I asked my Instagram followers, 'What makes a good friend?':

- Someone who respects your boundaries.
- Someone who celebrates the wins, and most importantly remembers to support you in your losses.
- They ask, they listen and they remember.
- Honesty.
- Someone who shows up when you need them, even if you don't/can't see them often.
- Mutual support, effort, love, kindness, encouragement, generosity and ideas.
- Someone who celebrates the small wins with you.
- Accepts and doesn't expect more than you can give.
- Understanding that a lack of contact isn't about them, it's about overwhelm.
- Respects your opinion, even when you don't agree.
- Listens to your shit without judgement or trying to fix it. Doesn't criticise decisions.

Friends don't have to be love at first sight

Sometimes we need to try new things a few times to see if they're a good fit, like trying a new sport, club or group. We might need a few goes to see if whatever (or whomever) is right. And the same applies to money. We can't try something for a week and write it off. We are trying to shift *years* of habits, methods and coping strategies. And so, when it comes to finding our people and our money solutions, it can be really helpful to think of the train analogy from Chapter 1 – there might be delays, shit passengers and expensive maintenance, but we can usually continue on the journey without decommissioning the whole train.

Whether we're looking for the right room of people or the right way to manage our money, we're on the journey with constant curiosity, and everything/everyone we find who isn't the right fit is one less thing to try.

How to work out who you actually like

A huge part of finding our people is working out what we like in people. To bring it back to our train metaphor, who are the passengers in our carriages, and who's sitting up front with the driver? While this sounds simple, in practice, it's a bloody nightmare. Relationships with people in our lives are more complicated than trigonometry, but lucky for you, I have a tidy equation that sums it all up:

$$\text{friend} = \frac{\sqrt{(YK \times 5) + (4qt / c) - 4}}{(v \times 6)}$$

If YK = years known, qt = quality time, c = commonalities and v = vibes, who is still my friend and why is this formula so complicated? I'm just kidding. Here's the truth: sometimes we keep people in our lives, even when it makes no sense, and sometimes things change for reasons that don't make much sense either. The good news? It only has to make sense to you. Not everyone has to be on your train for the same length of time. They can get on and off, they can get on at a later station; there are no rules.

The framework I use to make sense of who I keep in my life, why and to what extent is from *The Circles* by Kerry Armstrong. It proposes that there are seven circles that represent the seven levels of people who are involved in our life. You can shape the metaphor however you like. Maybe you'll have seven planets orbiting around your sun at different distances, seven train stations with you at the start of the route or even seven Tupperware containers stacked within each other. Importantly, the circles aren't fixed. People can pass in and out of them at different times of their lives and yours.

Regardless of how you picture your circles, the idea is to

understand how much energy to give people and their actions. I find it very cathartic. When someone brings out feelings in me, I consider what circle I would put them in at that time and process the feelings through that lens. Someone from circle seven is going to (hopefully) get less of my mental energy than someone in circle one. Here's an overview:

1. In the first circle, you have your soulmates, the people who know you best, who support you best and who you can trust. You can tell them anything without judgement. You can rely on their advice and they have your best interests at heart, which includes telling you hard truths when you might need to hear them. You might not have any people in the first circle, depending on where you're at in your journey, and that's okay.

2. In the second circle, you have good relationships. Loving them is easy, but they aren't soulmates. You enjoy spending time with them and it doesn't drain your energy.

3. In the third circle, you also have good people, but for whatever reason, they just aren't as close to people in the second circle. Maybe you're old friends who have drifted in different directions, or family you like but don't see often or know that well. Vibes are still good, just less strong.

4. The fourth circle has waiting room energy. It can work as a holding space – for people who are potentially moving outwards or inwards. Almost like quarantine, it gives people an opportunity to show symptoms (good or bad) before you make a decision about them.

5. The fifth circle is an interesting space. It's where you put people who you need to have some distance from without guilt. They aren't out, but they aren't in. Maybe they're people from your past who you don't connect with in the same way or don't have anything in common with. Maybe they're family members who you love but don't like very much. It's whatever you need it to be.

6. The sixth circle is for people who, for whatever reason, are there for necessity. It's hard to connect with these people, but you both need each other – not in a toxic way but in a practical way. Maybe they're your colleagues, housemates or friends of friends who you bump into regularly as part of life. Are you going to be rude? No. But do you vibe? Also no. Circle six allows you to mentally define your contact with these people without feeling any guilt or resentment in trying to self-explain your association with them.

7. Circle seven is a couple of things. It can be for people we need a break from, whether it's because of conflict, damage done or other pain points that have impacted the relationship. It can also be for self-protection, allowing you to consciously minimise contact and effort – for example, if they consistently breach your boundaries and cause you pain. It can also be for people who have exited your life and you still have grief about it and/or you still care about the person. You wish them all the best and still think about them, but they aren't in your day-to-day considerations, and you don't spend any time with them.

Your circles can be like your bank accounts – you can have as many or as few as you like. Maybe you have a Lindt ball – your soft centres and your outer shells. Maybe you have first class, business and economy. It's your system.

Whatever system you use, it gives you a framework for which passengers get on your train, for how long and how close they sit to the driver. Most importantly, it stops any guilt that comes up for not liking someone as much as you think they deserve, or for keeping someone in your life that everyone else around you (and maybe parts of yourself) really thinks doesn't belong there. It allows you to maintain different relationships with grace and carve space in the closer circles for those who deserve it. Simply, it allows you some space.

What about people who hate you?

People who hate you will always find a reason to hate you. Seriously, read that again. People who hate you will *always* find a reason to hate you. You could be solving world hunger and they'll still find a way.

This isn't unusual. I don't like everyone, and nor should I have to. Same for you. The other side of that coin is that we won't be liked by everyone. In fact, if everyone likes us, it generally means we've never put our neck out, never stood up for something, never disagreed with other people and never pissed anyone off at work. If we're liked by everyone, we have to wonder if we really like ourselves, since it sounds like we're putting everyone else first. How exhausting.

So, if haters are holding you back from a decision or living to your full potential … do it anyway. Because they'll find a way to hate you anyway, and we only get one shot to do something as a little blip on Earth, remember?

In a way, knowing you can never please everybody is really helpful when it comes to choosing your train tracks. There will never be anyone exactly like you or me ever again – not exactly. How can we truly compare ourselves with anyone else when we're not comparing the same things? Consider this:

- No one knows exactly who you know.
- No one knows exactly what you know.
- No one has experienced the same trauma that has made you who you are.
- No one likes exactly what you like.
- No one has the same relationships as you.
- No one has seen everything you've seen.

That means you have, in some way, a unique contribution to make to the universe. Statistically, this contribution probably isn't going to be world-changing. I spent five years ordering replacement toilet seats and telling people what colour their walls were painted. Was I changing the world? It didn't feel like it, but I was still supporting people I loved, some of whom were (and are) changing the world. Or supporting people who are, in turn, supporting people who are changing the world. I was still giving out into the world in my own small way. Maybe fixing someone's toilet or solving their annoying computer issue will give them the brain space to cure cancer. Who knows? Owning our uniqueness unapologetically gives other people the opportunity to do the same – and that does change the world.

Doner kebab

(takeaways) from Chapter 2

It's important to surround yourself with people who are compatible with your values, lifestyle and emotional needs. Your friends directly impact your quality of life, including your finances, so it's important to understand how they fit into your world. Maybe you don't have space for particular friends anymore – and that's okay.

———————

Not everybody will like you, but you shouldn't let the fear of other people's disapproval dictate where your train is going.

? Reflective questions

Which rooms do I feel like I can be myself in right now, and which make me feel uncomfortable?

Can I change the rooms I don't feel safe in, or can I spend less time in them?

What framework do I like for understanding my relationship levels? Circles, planets, Lindt balls or something else?

What circles would I put people around me into?

Does my time spent with people reflect their circle? Am I spending enough time with my first-circle relationships or too much with sixth- or seventh-circle relationships?

Have some people gone past their stop on my train?

Am I comfortable with some people not liking me?

Can I appreciate and accept that I have a unique contribution to make to the world? Why/why not?

Chapter 3

How to find happiness
(in a world that's going to hell in a handbasket)

CONTENT WARNING

To my readers struggling with mental illness, if you're at a stage in your journey where the goal is simply surviving and happiness is not a consideration, I get it. Skip this chapter and come back to it later – or not at all.

Your happiness doesn't have to look like anyone else's. I know it sounds like one of those cute but useless Instagram memes that people put on their story with no context, but it's true. And yet it can be difficult to work out what makes you happy and live a life aligned with what makes you happy. Achieving both is essential because it directly affects your money.

----

*Your happiness doesn't have
to look like anyone else's.*

More money ≠ more happiness

I know a dude, a very, very rich dude. Let's call him Frank. Frank is a family friend who has been retired for a long time, lives in a spectacular villa with city views and travels wherever he wants every year. Honestly, to look at Frank's life from the outside, you'd be convinced he'd nailed it.

Frank also happens to be one of the most miserable people I've ever met. He never has a good word to say. Whenever you see Frank, he's complaining about something or someone. It'd be hilarious if it wasn't so bloody sad.

As it happens, I have a few friends like this. They've got beautiful houses, posh cars, gorgeous-looking lives, but not happiness – or certainly not much of it. But I do have lots of friends who are happy without six bathrooms, a convertible or live-in staff. What I find fascinating, though, is they don't have a lot in common with each other.

Alison loves to bushwalk and teach choir. Dani is obsessed with good wine and Fringe World Festival Perth. My brother loves to coach volleyball and play Dungeons and Dragons. Steve and Ridhwaan love to cook and are obsessed with their cat, Mimi.

What these people have in common is that they don't think 'When I have more money I will enjoy this more.' These are people who, over time, have managed to fine-tune what makes them happy. Happiness is personal.

It's easy to get fixated on the future

We tend to think that when we have more money we'll be happier. We can fall into developing a mindset of 'I'll be happier when I have more money' without really defining how.

What is it about money that is actually going to make you happy (or happier)? What are the key areas where more money is going to substantially increase your happiness?

Obviously, money means you can meet your basic needs, which certainly increases your happiness. But once we get past the threshold of being able to meet basic housing, food and safety needs, we start paying the price for not knowing what makes us happy. While money can help you be happy, money is no guarantee you will be happy. I know a lot of people well into six figures a year who I would not describe as happy.

A few things are going on here. First, it's as though we postpone working out what makes us happy because we feel there's no point if we can't pay for it. Then, if our money situation improves, we look around and go 'Well, now what?' Second, we often let our lifestyle costs creep up, or we take out debt to spend on things we think are going to make us happy now (like an expensive 'simply couldn't miss it' Europe trip with friends you don't even hang out with anymore). Third, this debt might be for a seemingly essential purchase, such as a house.

The Great Australian Dream – or your nightmare

We've had the great property ownership dream drummed into us since we were in the womb. We save and save to purchase a place as early as possible so we can get into the property market. Then, all of a sudden, we are paying 30% to 60% of our income on a mortgage, plus council rates, insurance and strata fees. For some people, having property is the best decision of their lives. For other people, having property – the Great Australian Dream – can quickly become a nightmare.

But even when we're looking outside of the Great Australian Dream, it's so easy to fall into the trap of being 'inspired' (read: influenced) by people around us when we're trying to work out what makes us happy.

'Everyone always looks so happy on Instagram'

This shit started way before Instagram. You've probably heard the phrase 'keeping up with the Joneses'. It comes from *Keeping up with the Joneses*, a comic that ran from 1913 to 1940. It was based on a family trying to keep up with their more affluent neighbours. Keeping up, after all, is a form of fitting in.

When we don't know what makes us happy, we subconsciously look around for external markers of what potentially should. And in the age of no one talking to their neighbours but having everybody we've ever met become our friend on social media, happiness judged by an Instagram feed seems to be overseas trips, engagement rings, sold signs, baby bumps, the occasional boat, new jobs and attending multiple fancy events without wearing the same outfit. It's been a while since I saw anyone post a picture of themselves gardening, that's for sure.

When this is all we see on the surface, it's no surprise we think everyone else is happier than us. I've been shocked at how unhappy some people are once I've gotten to know them. You can never truly know if a person is happier than you, no matter what their life looks like or what they tell you. If you get caught in this trap, try to prove it to yourself. What evidence do you actually have that they are happier?

Staying in your lane

A huge part of knowing your worth is understanding what you value – and to work that out, you have to ignore what everyone else is doing. You also need to ignore what everyone else thinks about what you're doing, and why it's important to you.

Getting to know yourself – your priorities, your values, your goals, your joys – is like being on your train without having decided which destination is for you yet. Working out what makes *you* happy is how you start defining not only your destination but also your stations along the way and the passengers who need to get on (or off) your train. It's time to start practising the happiness you think you'll find when you have more money.

It's also important to know that your journey might be a bit uncomfortable. Maybe you've never actively thought about what makes you happy or interrogated why you think buying certain things will make you happy. It can be confronting, but it's worth it. The relationship you have with yourself will be the longest relationship of your whole life.

Luckily, you don't have to find all the answers overnight. Here are some examples of how to start practising happiness, no matter how far away you are from your lush wealth era.

Future 'wealth-energy' goals	How to practise
Travel	Try house swaps, staycations, camping, Airbnb overnighters three to four hours away, road trips, train trips, bus trips.
Designer stuff	Buy a good fake. Do you like it as much as you thought? Do you use it as much as you thought? Make a vision board on Pinterest of the ways you would style it. Can you come up with enough ways to justify the price per wear?
House	Start interrogating people you know when you go to their house. Dead set. What do they love? What would they change? What has surprised them about owning a home? Also, start going to open homes in your desired areas. You might be surprised by what you learn and what you actually like.
Convertible or fancy-schmancy car	Hire one for a couple of days – I'm deadly serious. You're thinking about dropping $80k+ on a depreciating asset. Make. Sure. Write a list of what you love about it. Are those things still going to be there in a second-hand version? Add ancillary costs such as insurance, servicing, detailing etc. Are you okay with maintaining a car that requires that level of care?

Future 'wealth-energy' goals	How to practise
Killer wardrobe	Swap clothes or go op-shopping. You can find inspiration on Instagram, TikTok, Pinterest or blogs. Something I've been doing is following accounts that focus on styling, especially re-styling the same pieces in different ways.
Gold Class every weekend	Really level up on the home cinema (even if it's just your laptop with a box over the top). Extra butter popcorn, champagne, $2 frozen Cokes from Maccas, chicken wings, Maltesers. Make it an *event*. Then try Gold Class. How does it compare to doing it at home in your pyjamas?
More time with your family (or yourself)	Negotiate a nine-day fortnight. Strategically use your annual leave around public holidays. Negotiate working from home one to two days a week. Run your own business? Have a 'professional development rest day' every month and close the office (your staff will love you, too). Separate your business and personal phone numbers – with an e-sim, for example – and turn off your business number when you aren't working.
Supporting your community	Start your wish list and open a bank account. Even if you can only put $5 a fortnight in there, you'll always have a bit available to help out. Start a list of ideas for meals or have a monthly cook-up night for whoever wants to come for a feed.

In the table following, I've added extra activities if you have no idea what happiness looks like for you (and seriously, don't underestimate the easy or 'boring' stuff). It includes heaps of things my friends like, although I have no idea why they do them (proof again that happiness is personal). You can also do short courses to see if something is for you before you start spending big money.

Extra activities

Reading	Going on picnics
Gardening	Baking bread
Listening to a podcast while walking	Volunteering
	Sewing
Practising yoga/Pilates	DIY spa day with hydrating face masks and pedicures – you can get the kids involved too
Going to games nights	
Swimming	
Writing	Paint-by-numbers
Beer brewing	Dance classes
Joining a choir	Wine tasting
Cooking	Lifting weights
Crafting	Heading out for coastal drives
Playing chess online	Checking out art exhibitions
Listening to classical music	Flower arranging
Running	Making cocktails or coffee

Are you starting to see how your money has little to do with happiness but how your happiness has a lot to do with money? It's not about spending less; it's about spending in the right direction.

If you don't enjoy travel but enjoy the security of owning your own home, a $3000 mortgage repayment is a good happiness alignment for you. Conversely, if you love to travel, spending $1000 a month on renting a room in a share house and freeing up $2000 for a Japan trip might be more your vibe. The amount of money spent is the same, but the happiness gained is totally different.

Maybe you're spending $500 a month on beauty and wardrobe upkeep for your corporate job, but what you secretly want to do is drop a day a week and launch a YouTube cooking channel, start a dog-walking business or discover what the hell it is you *do* want.

If you're dissatisfied with your life, chances are that feeling won't go away with a pay rise. It's worth discovering what makes you happy now. Sometimes, you'll find that a lot of what makes you happy is actually really cheap.

Case study: Julio, 39

I was at a friend's place for dinner and we got chatting about the year ahead. I asked him if he had any travel plans. 'No,' he said, 'travel isn't important to me.' 'That's cool,' I replied. 'Tell me what *is* important to you?'

It turns out Julio was working long shifts in a fly-in, fly-out job to buy a number of investment properties. Why? So he could use the money from those assets to buy and fix vintage cars while still having the properties grow in value.

On being happy when the world is going to hell in a handbasket

In the space of 100 years, we've gone from hearing the news once a day through newspapers or radio to receiving news stories from every corner of the globe every second. Extreme weather events, wars, school shootings, suicide rates and domestic family violence ... it's no secret that negative news sells.

Now, more than ever, we are super aware of how terrible things are for other people. While this means we're better placed than ever to help others, sometimes it feels kind of ... icky to be focused on finding happiness when the world is both literally and metaphorically burning around us. It can feel audacious going to art galleries, getting a massage or even spending time quietly resting.

However, not taking care of ourselves limits our capacity to care for others. Have you ever noticed when you're tired, unhappy or worn out, you have much less to give to those around you? I know that when I'm in that state, my temper and patience are shorter, and I find it much harder to be unselfish and think about anyone but myself. When I'm rested – whether through actual rest, or through spending time on things that make me happy – I'm much more able to care, and give.

Finding a few moments of happiness is restorative. Knowing what makes us happy and doing those things allows us to protect ourselves and lend support to those close or far while keeping our own gravity centred.

So yes, the world is going to hell in a handbasket. But the handbasket has tassels on it and there are snacks inside. It's time to work out what snacks you like.

Chicken katsu bowl

(takeaways) from Chapter 3

More money does not guarantee more happiness.

Comparing yourself to others, especially based on their public lifestyle, will never serve you.

Waiting for some ideal future before doing things that make you happy is a waste of the present. There are ways you can enjoy happiness now.

Finding your happiness will give you the energy and capacity to support others.

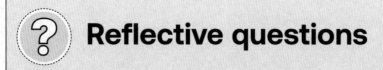

Reflective questions

Who do I know who is really happy? Why?

Do I know anyone who's miserable, even though their life looks amazing? Why?

Am I happy? Why/why not?

When do I feel happy? Why? What am I doing?

What am I doing when I feel most enraged or annoyed? Can I spend money to solve that problem?

What hobbies did I do or want to do when I was young? Why did I stop or not do them?

What do I wish I had more time for?

What makes me envious of other people? Why?

What causes would I like to support if I had the time and/or money to do so?

Chapter 4

Relationships

The Harvard Study of Adult Development has run one of the longest 'happiness studies' in the world. With over 700 participants and running for 85 years, the study tracked the same people for decades – and found that the most significant indicator of a happy life in participants was loving relationships. So not only is this chapter a piece in the money puzzle, but it also has life-shaping importance. It covers how your relationships affect your money, whether you're single or in an intimate relationship. (For my non-monogamous friends, please adjust 'partner' to 'partners' where I haven't already done so.)

Why our relationships matter for our money

Our relationships drastically affect our money – both from a literal perspective and an emotional perspective. It was one of the most consistent themes that came through my financial counselling and coaching door. Here is a selection of examples:

Situation	Consequence
Needing to support a parent/child/sibling with money.	Relationships ending because of loans not being paid back.

Situation	Consequence
Needing to reduce work hours to support a sick family member.	Tension between siblings when one has supported a parent and others haven't.
Leftover debt from an intimate relationship that has ended.	Bitterness when comparing financial position to the financial positions of friends or family who are in healthy intimate relationships.
Gambling illness or other addiction in the family.	Financial loss from supporting a person with addiction; relationship breakdown when a person with addiction is not ready to make change; resentment from other family members towards both the person with the addiction and anyone providing financial support to them.
Struggling financially as a couple in the early days of the relationship.	One partner still working long hours years later, despite now being financially comfortable, causing resentment and feelings of neglect.
Being expected to always pick up the tab as the 'high earner' friend.	Turning down invitations and events to avoid dealing with the expectation, or to avoid having the hard conversation.
Family gifting or lending a deposit, or going guarantor on a loan.	Their help being leveraged or weaponised into "If it wasn't for us ..."

We cannot separate our money – how we spend it, how we save it, how we think about it – from our relationships. The more contentment and emotional support we develop in our relationships, the less we use money as a crutch, or as the hinge by which we determine the quality of our relationships. Our relationships are, of course, also intertwined with finding our people, connecting with our values, living our own authentic timeline and finding our happiness. But let's start with the most important relationship first.

Our relationship with ourselves

At the centre of the seven circles from Chapter 2 is you. You are – and always will be – your longest relationship. You may as well embrace it and work at it. How you see yourself, speak to yourself and treat yourself shapes what you tolerate from others, but also how you spend your money. When you have a good relationship with yourself, you can identify if your spending is coming from need, emotional or external influences, or if you're buying something just for you.

Here are a few examples of what a 'still developing' and 'developed' relationship with yourself looks like:

Still developing	Developed
Avoiding or soothing feelings by spending (or other habits).	Acknowledging and processing feelings.
Not resting – over-exercising or over-committing to plans and events.	Scheduling/taking time for rest, understanding capacity and not over-committing yourself.
Hating being alone, or becoming restless.	At peace or even revelling in being alone.
Hanging out with people you don't like out of obligation or a desire to be connected.	Spending time with quality people and having strong boundaries; possibly fewer but more wholesome relationships.

We've already talked about finding out what makes you happy and finding your room, and in Chapter 11, we'll be talking about how to be your own financial coach and support yourself from a money-and-feelings perspective. What we haven't talked about, however, are two very important aspects of your relationship with yourself: dating yourself and boundaries.

Honey, are you dressed for dinner?

It's time to set the standard of how you want to be treated – by doing it yourself. Whether you have a partner, want to be partnered or are content being single, there is nothing more powerful than creating incredible experiences with yourself.

This fits in with everything we've already discussed. Want to find better rooms? Try new things where you're forced to make conversation. Want to find out what happiness looks like to you? Test the waters. If you want to know who you are, in values, in life and in money, you will need to spend time with yourself in a purposeful way. Sure, working out and chilling in bed watching movies is spending time with yourself, but it's not active engagement. It doesn't provide space for intentional self-reflection or personal introspection.

Enter dating. It's hard to overstate the power of dating yourself. It's scary good, and it builds your ability to give zero fucks. Take yourself for dinner. I found dinner to be the scariest one in the beginning because it has a different tone to popping somewhere for lunch. But now it's my favourite. I do it a few times a year, including my birthday, and always go somewhere decent. I dress to impress my date (me), order whatever I want and just … hang out. I keep off my phone. Sometimes I take a notebook, but not always. I think about things. I relax. It's the best. It forces you to be a bit uncomfortable in the beginning – people will likely give you weird looks for going out to a traditionally social activity by yourself – but you'll develop the phenomenal skill of realising when you're not having a good time with other people.

If there's anything you wish you had in your current relationship or that you want in a future relationship, start setting the bar. If you're happy being single, do all the things that we're told by society are 'better together'. Trips away? I met one of my best friends when I was on a weekend away by myself. Movies are an easy one, as you're in the dark for three hours. Go Gold Class (or have your fancy at-home equivalent!). Hiking, fishing, cycling. Once you've experienced the luxury of not compromising, it really does change the game.

Buying yourself things is also part of dating yourself. Buy yourself flowers. Get your nails done as a date rather than as an efficient appointment. Hell, add a pedicure. Go to a cafe and sit in an armchair reading and drinking fancy coffee while sneakily people-watching for three hours. Do all the 'significant other' things that society has conditioned you to expect from someone else – even if you have a significant other.

Ideally, you're not using 'dating myself' as an excuse to mindlessly buy things all the time. Instead, you're purposefully using your money to do things that make you feel loved, like if you were dating your dream person. For example, when dating myself, I quickly realised that buying flowers was iconic, but that I hated the movies. I loved dinners, but getting my nails done was a poor time investment when I didn't really enjoy it. Getting the house cleaned so I don't have to do it? That's me dating me, baby. No one becomes the love of your life without winning you over. So win yourself over.

Keep your boundaries strong

The grass stays greener when you don't let people park their cars on it for weeks at a time. Boundaries are what help us make sure people don't overstay their welcome, whether that's physically or emotionally.

Boundaries go two ways: setting and keeping yours, and respecting other people's.

Boundaries can be a protective tool for the person setting them, but they are also an enabling tool. They enable us to keep people in our lives, and to keep our minds healthy. If you haven't grown up with good boundary role modelling, setting and responding to healthy boundaries will probably feel entirely awful. It's pretty confronting having to communicate your needs clearly, or having someone communicate their needs with you. But, like dating yourself, you have to get comfortable with the uncomfortable, and it gets easier with practice.

The boundaries will vary depending on what circle the person is in, or if it's worth the fight when it comes to certain people.

I could spend this whole book discussing boundaries, so instead I'll share some examples of voicing your boundaries and recommend my favourite book on boundaries: *The Joy of Being Selfish: Why You Need Boundaries and How to Set Them* by Michelle Elman.

Money boundaries

Here are some examples of how you can establish a money boundary in a way that is honest and unapologetic, without being mean or rude:

- 'The last few times we've split the cheque equally as a group, and I'm feeling frustrated as I don't drink. Can we split the food between five of us and the alcoholic drinks between four?'
- 'That's out of budget for me at the moment. Can we save that and do something else this time?'
- 'I can't put in that amount for the joint present. I can put in XXX, or I'm happy to get something just from me.'
- 'That activity isn't for me, but I'll do my best to get to the next thing.'

Personal boundaries

Here are some ways boundaries can be set, outside of money conversations:

- 'I'm not talking about my weight/partner/gender today.'
- 'Please don't vape in my car.'
- 'I don't have capacity to speak to you every day. I can do a few texts during the week, or a call one night.'
- 'If you aren't going to be home for dinner, text and let me know. If you aren't willing to communicate your movements, we'll have dinner without waiting, and you can put something together for yourself when you get home.'

Respecting other people's boundaries

Respecting boundaries can be confronting and feel like an attack. It's hard to remember that the boundary isn't personal; it's a protective feature to enable that person to have the best relationship they can with you. Respecting other people's boundaries is essential to maintaining close relationships, and by extension, your long-term happiness. Very briefly, here's what responding to boundaries looks like:

- Not justifying ('Oh, but I just did it because …').
- Thanking them for telling you.
- Acknowledging if you can meet that boundary. If you can't meet that boundary, ask if you can work with the person to find an alternative.
- Asking for clarification if needed ('I have a couple of questions about XXX boundary. Is it okay if I text them to you now or do you want me to wait?').
- Managing your reactions to their boundary. If you need to take some time to process what the request brings up for you, let them know that and when you'll be back in touch. It's okay to have an emotional reaction to a boundary, but it's not okay to let that reaction shape your reply.

Importantly, keep in mind how hard it likely was for that person to set or express that boundary. Be kind, and take your time. My psychologist friend Madonna Salem recommends understanding your own attachment style to give yourself understanding and grace in how you react. It also helps with understanding how people might react to your boundaries. A book we both love is *Attached: The New Science of Adult Attachment and How It Can Help You Find – and Keep – Love* by Amir Levine and Rachel SF Heller.

The romance of friendships

It's time to end the separation between 'relationship' and 'friendship'. Don't even get me started on the word 'platonic'.

Friendships – everything from casual friends to 'chosen family' to colleagues to gym besties and high school friends – truly make the world go round.

Just because you aren't having sex with someone doesn't mean your relationship isn't romantic or intimate. While this can refer to your partner/s, it can also apply to all your relationships. Our friendships are romantic, glorious, intimate. Sometimes a friendship is a passionate fling that burns out quickly. Sometimes it's a slow burn. Sometimes it's long distance. And sometimes it's forever.

Still don't believe me? The definition of romance is a feeling of mystery and excitement associated with love. Intimacy is defined as a cosy, private or relaxed atmosphere. I've heard plenty of romance and intimacy in the way my friends and I speak to each other, such as:

- 'Tell me everything.'
- 'What ever happened to that colleague of yours who stole the …'
- 'Take that garlic bread out of the oven for me so I can keep talking.'
- 'OMG, you will never guess who I saw last week.'
- 'Babe, grab that blanket.'
- 'I'm coming in my pyjamas.'
- 'Bring your wine to the couch.'
- 'Peppermint or chamomile?'
- 'What do you think about the Teals proposal to …?'
- 'Have you read this book?'
- 'I saw this and thought of you immediately.'
- 'Do you want to come to this flower festival with me?'

If I didn't tell you my friends and I say these things, it'd be natural to assume it was my partner, right? Good friends will outlive most (if not all) of your romantic relationships. Treat them accordingly and …

Tell people that you love them

For every 'I love you' someone says without hearing it back, 0.001 millimetres of the ozone layer gets repaired. Did I make that statistic up? Yes. Do I think it could be accurate? Also yes.

There are lots of people who don't feel safe saying 'I love you', whether that's to everyone, only some people, or most people. It might be from trauma, fear or embarrassment, or they simply weren't brought up that way. It's a terrifying thing to say to someone – but it shouldn't be.

We need to shift the tone behind 'I love you'. Rather than 'I love you' being a huge, romantic, life-altering commitment, the end of the scene where one person is getting on a plane, it should be like the dusting of icing sugar on a cake. It doesn't change the taste, but it adds a little something.

I once had an older client with hearing loss who was also quite forgetful. I never quite got the whole story, but she was estranged from most of her family. They drifted in and out and she didn't get on very well with them. She used to call me a lot, and because of her hearing loss, I had to shout to be heard. One time, after we finished up, she goes, 'Alright, love you, darling.'

I could have remained utterly professional, laughed it off awkwardly and told her I'd see her soon. 'LOVE YOU TOO, JOSEPHINE,' I belted in response. The entire IT department across the hall turned around, looked at me, looked at each other and shook their heads.

If you have love to spare, give it to anyone who needs it. Why should we gatekeep our love, or reserve it for people who only attain a certain level of our affection?

Something I use a lot is the 'love you, bye'. My friends and I normally say it as one word – 'loveyoubye'. We say it when we're ending a phone call, on the last hug before we leave each other, when we bump into each other somewhere – whenever. It's more casual, less intimate, but still counts. It's a lovely introduction to 'love yous', if you need it, though definitely not to be confused with 'love youse'.

It's fine if people don't say it back

There is such joy in saying 'I love you' without needing to hear it back. I have quite a few friends who don't say 'I love you' back, for whatever reason, but I don't let it bother me, because I *know* they love me. Here's how I know:

- They cook for me.
- They message and ask specific questions about things we spoke about last time we hung out.
- They call.
- We talk about how grateful we are to know each other.
- They genuinely listen.

What is love if not the romance and intimacy that comes from knowing a person and what matters to them? You might have to be the one who says it first. Of course, in some cultures, it's much less common and acceptable to say 'I love you', so bear in mind that some of your friends (or you) might feel less comfortable saying it or saying it back.

Plus, a lot of my male friends are super panicked when I say 'loveyoubye', and I blame toxic masculinity and the patriarchy for that. I do it anyway, appreciate they might not ever say it back, and just say it very lowkey – not staring into their eyes, just as a casual throwaway. I'd rather say 'loveyoubye' and never hear it back versus one of us getting hit by a bus and regretting that I didn't say it.

Want good relationships? Listen up.

It was life-changing when I realised some people didn't need or want me to tell them what to do. They just needed to tell me how they were feeling and get it off their chest.

This revelation came to me when I was going through a couple of emotionally gross situations at the same time, but I simply wasn't ready to do anything about them. Some friends gave me advice I didn't want and some just listened. I noticed and appreciated the difference and made sure I did the same – and it levelled up my friendships immensely.

You can do this in a few ways. You can ask the person who is talking about the problem, 'Is it better for me to just listen, or do you want some advice too?' Another very blunt one is 'sympathy or solutions?', which is a good one when you have a lot of rapport and are used to asking each other for the boundary.

It's also important to listen without spending the whole time mentally planning what you want to say about it. You can tell when a person is listening to respond rather than listening to hear. They nod very quickly like they're waiting for you to finish. They interrupt you, or they're ready with a 'yes, but' or a 'yes, and' without even taking a breath after your sentence. Contrast this with a friend who pauses, reflects back to you ('So you're saying that …'), or asks thoughtful follow-up questions first.

People love to be heard and asked meaningful questions. Once you start paying attention to how this happens to you, or how you do it to others, it will start to support the other work you're doing – choosing your train tracks, finding your tofu room and drawing your relationship circles.

Plus, when we're heard and understood, it helps us to soothe and heal, which in turn allows us to rely less on spending money (or rigorously controlling our money) as a coping tool.

What about when listening isn't enough?

I always had a goal at work: I didn't need people to leave my session feeling better; but I did want them to leave 'not feeling any worse'. This is a fantastic tool when you have a friend who is sharing a hard or emotional situation with you. Have you ever had someone ask you 'Is there anything I can do?' and find it too overwhelming in the context of what you're going through? I certainly have. 'Is there anything I can do that won't make it worse?' is a lowkey way of asking and making yourself available while acknowledging that the situation is bad and you don't want to cause more harm.

Talk about money with your friends

Keeping our money fears and questions in the dark helps no one. Be the friend who starts bringing money conversations to the table. You and your friends will be better for it, whether it's 'What are you saving for at the moment?' or 'How much are your mortgage repayments? I'm trying to work out what I can afford.' If you aren't ready to be the conversation starter, find a room where it's already on the table and pull up a chair. Practise listening. You'll be surprised by what you learn.

Just because a friendship ends, doesn't mean it was a failure

Sometimes relationships go out with a bang, sometimes they drift apart at sea and sometimes they just die a natural death. It doesn't matter if you've been friends for a year, ten years or 30 years, we simply cannot expect to grow in the same direction. Friendships serve you for as long as they serve you, and whether or not you wish the person well after your friendship ends, it's an ending, not a failure.

Remember, you get to choose the passengers on your train. And if some of them need to get off at stations as you go – wish them well (even if you hate their guts) and keep doing you. You should always have a destination in mind, and if the same passengers come with you all the way, all the better. But it's *your* destination.

Letting go of friendships (or being the one left behind) can be tough, but you can do hard things, and you'll become better for it.

Family relationships

All the advice for friendships stays true for our family relationships (blood or chosen). Our family relationships are powerful influences on our money habits and beliefs, which we'll talk about in Part 2 and Part 3. They test our money boundaries and shape our goals. Teasing apart how our familial relationships have impacted or are impacting our money is often lifelong work. Much of this work is around setting and respecting boundaries, identifying patterns and deciding if we want to continue or change those patterns. In many cultures, financially supporting family is expected, and even when it's not expected, we can put that pressure on ourselves.

Case study: Amani, 52

Amani came to financial counselling with rent and utilities overdue. While completing her statement of financial position (income and expenses sheet), it became clear some expenses were higher than they should be for her and her adult son (who still lived at home).

Amani was paying the phone bill for her two other adult children who had moved out of home and was substantially subsidising their food costs as well as her own.

It was a hard conversation to have. Amani felt incredibly guilty about exposing her children to family violence while they were young, and the way she atoned for that was to continue to provide large amounts of financial support. In the meantime, she was leaving herself at a disadvantage and at risk of being evicted or having her power disconnected.

There were so many factors to work through – Amani's guilt over letting her children down, her embarrassment at having to tell them why she had to reduce her support, and the fear of what would happen if she didn't have the conversation.

We put some arrangements in place for her rent and utilities in the short-term, and having that sorted gave Amani some mental space to have a conversation with her kids who, once they under-stood the situation, quickly organised to take ownership of their own expenses.

Family boundaries and influences can take years to process, let alone improve. If this is you, be patient and curious about the process. A lot of my clients found that support from a counsellor or psychologist was a much-needed addition to the financial process when working through this.

'Intimate relationships'

No, I haven't talked about this in detail for a couple of reasons. Firstly, I don't think the advice should be that different from that for friendships, and secondly, I don't think it's the most important relationship of your life (sorry, not sorry). I put intimate relationships last because they're often the first thing (sometimes the only thing) talked about when it comes to relationships and money. And while it's important, it's not as important as you and your inner circles.

All my advice about finding your people, setting boundaries and mourning an endpoint without treating it as a failure also applies to intimate relationships. The divorce rate is 44% in Australia for a reason. Love that lasts forever is rare, and, in my opinion, should be the exception rather than the expectation. Of the long-term intimate relationships you know, how many of them are truly happy? Sure, some – I know a few. But that number also decreases with the length of time. There's a big difference between a five-year long-term relationship and a 20-year long-term relationship. We need to stop treating separation like it's a failure and more like it's the end of a guest star's run on a TV series. Sure, a character may have exited, but the show hasn't ended.

Of course, there are a couple of extra financial considerations for those of us who are in intimate relationships. If you are building a life with someone, there are two key pieces of advice I can give you from seeing the good, bad and very ugly come through the door over the years.

Talk about money early

This doesn't have to start with a full sit-down planning meeting of future goals and joint accounts, though it can be if you want. It can be as simple as asking what your intimate partner is saving for, noticing what they like to spend on or asking their advice on money decisions you're going to make.

Here are some questions you might like to think about:

- Are they reckless or conservative with their money? How does that sit with you?
- Are they vaguely familiar with their financial position, such as what they have going in and out? Do they have savings? Do they have financial goals or plans, or do they live in the moment? Is that going to work for you, both now and in five years? In 20 years?
- Do they talk about money, or are they private about it?

None of these are inherently good or bad. It's just good to notice how they make *you* feel in terms of security and compatibility.

Protect yourself

Sometimes it can be difficult to tell if someone is having a difficult money conversation with you, or is deliberately weaponising the money conversation to shift themselves into a position of control or power. Here are some subtle red flags to keep an eye out for:

- Do they criticise your decisions and undermine what you choose to do with your money?
- Do they suggest you combine all your money because they will manage it much better than you?
- Do they ask you to account for everything you spend in a joint account, in detail?
- Do they make comments about how 'bad with money' you are?
- Do they decide the 'joint' goals?
- Do they pay all the bills without letting you see or know how much they are?
- Do they put joint bills in your name alone?
- Do they roll their eyes and shake their head when you talk about money you've spent or deals you scored?

You might be thinking 'Hang on, my partner/s and I do some of these and I feel totally, absolutely safe with it.' Yes, it's okay if one or two of these work for you. But if you're reading that list and feeling uncomfortable, anxious or icky about things that are on it and how they might apply to you, chances are there's a problem.

We're going to talk about economic abuse and coercive control in more detail in Part 2, but for now, keep in mind that these are not healthy relationship behaviours. If you're worried you may be experiencing economic abuse, I want to emphasise that it's not your fault. It happens slowly over time, to the point where you don't even notice the gradual changes. You are not stupid. This happens *far* more than you might think. Fortune favours the prepared, and having these in the back of your mind might allow you to catch it earlier.

Consider your options, and if you'd like support, call 1800RESPECT and/or see a financial counsellor to have a confidential chat.

Keep some money separate

I'm very firm on my position that people should always have some money separate when they are in a relationship. This is for two reasons: your safety and your autonomy.

Your safety

Fully combined finances are more trouble than they're worth, trust me. It's not just about protecting yourself from economic abuse. For one thing, if you're a signatory to a bank account in your partner's name and your partner dies, the bank can lock the accounts until they get the paperwork they need under estate and probate requirements. I often had clients whose partners – often suffering from a gambling illness, drug addiction or mental illness – drained their joint accounts. Don't get me started on the affairs or 'sudden separations' where one partner leaves and cleans out the bank accounts. The family court process to get that money back is beyond belief. These situations are common horrors that are easily preventable.

Please, keep some money for yourself, whether it's in the open, in a secret account or in an envelope under your mum's cutlery tray. Generally, in a healthy partnership, having your own bank account should be an absolute non-issue.

Your autonomy (your 'self')

Every partner should have money they get to spend, without it being on a joint transaction statement. Maybe it's a KFC-after-work moment or a bought-a-lotto-ticket moment. Each person needs a safe space to spend money on things they love that aren't necessarily valued by the other partner/s. I love and condone having joint goals and joint expenses, and we'll talk about running systems that reflect that in Part 3. I understand the need for joint debts, such as mortgages. But I believe we need the freedom that comes from having money that is just our own.

Spicy ramen

(takeaways) from Chapter 4

Start identifying when some of your thoughts and behaviours are coming from a place of a 'still developing' or a 'developed' relationship with yourself.

———————

Set the standard of how you want to be treated by doing it yourself.

———————

Practise setting boundaries by starting with easier people or setting smaller ones ('I'm not talking about that today' versus 'I'm not talking about that ever again').

———————

Practise listening to hear instead of listening to respond.

———————

Give some thought to a nice way you can bring money conversations to the table. Sometimes it's easier to ask for advice (even if we might not take it).

———————

Tell people that you love them, even if they don't say it back.

———————

It's okay if we haven't untangled all the ways we've been impacted financially by our family influences, but working at it will help.

———————

Start talking about money with your partner, and reflect on how their answers make you feel in terms of financial security and compatibility.

———————

Keep some money separate.

Reflective questions

Can I identify any spending themes that stem from certain relationships?

What emotional impacts from relationships am I already conscious of?

How's my relationship with myself? Do I feel like I'm still developing, developed or a combination of both?

Do I like being by myself? Why/why not?

What kinds of things do I wish a partner would do for me?

What are some of my ideal dates?

What are my ideal gifts or acts of service?

What are some things I can do to show myself the love I deserve?

How is my boundary-setting?

Are there some people I find harder to set boundaries with than others? Why?

How do I respond to other people's boundaries?

Which of my friendships do I consider romantic? Why/why not?

When was the last time I told someone I loved them?
How do I feel about that?

Do I listen to hear or do I listen to respond?

Which of my friends seem to really listen to me? What is the difference?

Are there any ended friendships I haven't been able to move past? Why?

How do I feel about my partner's or partners' attitudes to money and money habits?

Will my partner/s and I be compatible in the long-term, or am I in the honeymoon period? Are there any red flags in how they talk to me about money?

Do I keep some money separate? If not, why not?

Chapter 5

The intersection between your money and yourself

Do you have money hang-ups? Maybe you've avoided everything to do with money because you don't feel like you have the skills. Maybe you've *always* had to do the money stuff in your relationship or family and carried other people's expectations as well as your own. Maybe you worry that if you don't tightly control your money, you'll lose it all.

These attitudes form when we're young, when we experience different types of trauma and are otherwise vulnerable. And we can carry them around for decades, wondering, 'Am I the only person like this?'

I can tell you now you're not. Everyone has money 'stuff'– and I mean everyone. CEOs, big business owners, celebrities. Singles, couples, throuples. Some people have enough money to mask their money stuff better, but everyone has it. And it's super important to acknowledge it and fix it for our own sake.

Stop punishing yourself (and your wallet)

When we're not healing our relationships with ourselves and others, it's easy for our money to be the punching bag. Similarly, if we're consumed by how stressful our money is, it impacts our relationships with family and friends, as well as our self-worth.

I've seen it in many financial counselling clients. They've been doing their best for so long, but they come in so defeated and unable to see the strengths they've demonstrated trying to manage their situation. They are so ashamed of what has happened to them (often it's not even their fault) that they haven't told anyone. The chaos is often fixable, but the work of helping that person see their own strengths and move forward in their situation is by far the hardest part – and often there are people who come back through financial counselling again because they haven't been able to address the underlying cause and the feelings that go with it.

Our trauma isn't our fault, but it *is* our responsibility to heal

Yes, that sentence is the best-worst truth there is. It is absolutely trash that things happen to us that we now need to fix. But the good news is that you can take all the credit for your healing.

Many of my financial counselling and coaching clients had issues with money that stemmed back to their relationships with themselves and/or other people. Building money confidence is a forever journey. Like our relationships, it is something to be improved rather than solved. It's understanding that there will be times when we go backwards or sideways in our relationships, whether that's the relationship with ourselves, others or our money. But it's also understanding that even when it's messy or we make mistakes, we deserve to feel worthy and confident about ourselves, our relationships with others, and our relationship with money.

Self-worth vs self-confidence

Self-worth is about your intrinsic (essential) belief that you deserve the basic emotional experiences of a human – to be loved, respected, valued. Self-confidence is trusting your skills and abilities and the way you present them to the world. It's the difference between nailing a job interview because you know you have the skills and the experience, but not trusting that your colleagues respect you or like you as a person. It's the difference between dressing however you want and owning it versus trusting that people will find you worthy of their time and respect, regardless of what you're wearing. It's knowing that you deserve people around you who love and respect you, and setting strong boundaries with people who don't.

Getting our money's worth

Getting our money's worth doesn't mean making every dollar go as far as it can. Absolutely not. However, if you're at that stage (either by choice or necessity – I see you), go for gold. It means getting what we value out of our money. It means getting to know what is important to us and what we want out of life so we can use money to maximise joy. This is not the same as the joy other people believe we need to see in our lives, or the joy we've been made to believe is 'right'. That's why your self-worth is so important in getting your money's worth.

Scarcity

In the book *Scarcity: Why Having Too Little Means So Much*, Sendhil Mullainathan and Eldar Shafir talk about the concept of bandwidth. Put simply, each human only has a certain amount of bandwidth. Think of it like a Frank Green water bottle, or a jar. You can only fill it to the top. Things that take up bandwidth look different for everyone. For example, for someone on or under the poverty line, it might look like trying to pay the electricity bill while organising back-to-school booklists, dealing with a broken heater and trying to feed five people on $40 a week. When you're in this position, easy financial choices become complex.

Case study: Lila, 35

Lila was a single mum with four kids, one of whom had a cognitive disability. Lila was on Parenting Payment and Family Tax Benefit. Every fortnight was a struggle, and she had a number of debts on payment arrangements. Lila chose to get her Family Tax Benefit annually rather than fortnightly (a lot of parents do this to help with stuff like car registration, holiday season etc.).

Lila came in after she got her lump sum to see if we could make some reduced offers to settle and clear some debts. She told me she used some of the money to buy her eldest Nike Jordans. Could we have used that money to make better offers? Sure. But at the end of the day, Lila was a mum who had a million things on her mind and a kid who desperately wanted shoes to fit in, and she, for once, had some money to do that.

Scarcity makes people do things that seem like bad financial decisions. But we've all been in situations where our brains have been so full that we can't seem to make any decision, let alone the right one. Scarcity creates a constant environment of 'full brain' for a person, including financially. They are operating in the best way they know how.

Scarcity can include dealing with a mental health or physical health crisis – yours or someone else's. It can be single parenting. It can be a toxic job where you put in 70 hours a week. Money doesn't exist in a vacuum.

Let's use the jar as an example. In the jar are some big rocks, stones and pebbles. The big rocks are your big energy drains – hard to move, hard to work around and consuming a lot of your daily energy quota. Your jar might look like this:

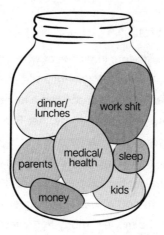

A year from now, it might look like this:

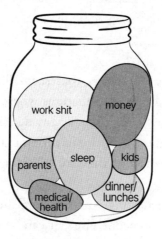

Our capacity to engage with our money will not only depend on whatever else we have going on, but it'll also ebb and flow over time. You can't plan your savings goal if you're getting help for a partner with a gambling illness or organising a funeral. The jar is a helpful way of assessing external factors that impact our money choices without too much criticism. We'll talk about this in detail in Chapter 12.

Salmon sushi hand roll

(takeaways) from Chapter 5

Everyone has money hang-ups.
Understanding and taking ownership of yours
will go a long way in helping you heal.

———————

Your relationship with yourself, others and money won't follow
a linear path of progression – and that's okay.

———————

Making good choices can be difficult when you're going
through a rough patch, but do your best with what you have.

 # Reflective questions

What are my money hang-ups? Where might they have come
from?

Do I have a sense of self-worth?

Do I have a sense of self-confidence?

What's in my brain jar? What's taking up the most space?
How can I make space?

Chapter 6

Trauma, the demons sitting on the shoulders of your money

Money books often talk about 'money stories' – core memories or experiences, usually from when we're young, that shape our money behaviours. Those core memories are often different from one person to the next, and their impact can vary even between siblings who grew up in the same household. Here are some examples from my financial coaching clients:

Core memory	Adult playout 1	Adult playout 2
Not enough food on the table.	Often buys way too much and hoards food and household items. Finds it hard to stick to a grocery budget.	Maintains a militant food budget with strict meal planning and execution.
Shared bedroom/ small living spaces/ regular moving.	Weakness for bedding, homewares and nesting.	Aversion to settling or only buying bare minimum furnishings.
Financial tension from a parent/ caregiver or between parents/ caregivers around debt.	Avoiding debt.	Leaning into debt as it's familiar.
Lots of holidays as a family.	Finding it difficult to live the same standard of lifestyle from childhood – possibly relying on debt.	Not wanting to travel (if experiences were negative).
Parent(s)/ caregiver(s) owning a property or properties.	Focusing on getting into the property market as early as possible, sometimes regardless of other goals.	Aversion/not wanting to own property.
Shared resources between families and/or community.	Giving too much to people who don't have the same reciprocation value.	Resenting the community expectation of sharing financial resources.

Core memory	Adult playout 1	Adult playout 2
Parent(s) or caregiver(s) are inclusive and open in money decisions for the household.	Higher understanding of financial products and banking and finding money decisions easy to navigate.	Confusion when discussing other people's money decisions and struggles to empathise.
Parent(s)/caregiver(s) understand investing and/or actively invest.	Willing to give investing a go and having an understanding of how investing builds wealth.	Confusion as to why everyone else isn't doing what you're doing as it makes so much sense.

Nothing on this list should make us feel bad about behaviour responses. They aren't negative things by default. Understanding the impact of core memories allows us to have compassion and curiosity for things we do with money that we find frustrating as adults or that don't seem logical – either to people around us or even to ourselves.

For example, a person who had a financially unstable childhood can find it very difficult to adopt a regular money routine after living through feast and famine in their early years. If they experience financial instability as an adult through job loss, a relationship ending or injury, they may panic, even if they have savings to support them. They can also find it difficult to spend money on expensive, quality items, and spending that much in a lump sum can bring up a visceral fear of not having enough for other things (yes, even if they have plenty of savings). Trauma can happen at any stage of life, though – it's not just what happens in early childhood. It can be in your university years, or middle age.

Case study 1: Jing, 41

Jing was a financial coaching client who, after spending years in an economically abusive relationship, was told they were bad with money and that the other partner needed to manage it so it didn't get out of control.

When we explored what they used to be like with money before they met their partner, they had memories of being good with money, always saving, paying for trips in cash etc. They had developed new core memories from years of being convinced they couldn't be trusted.

Case study 2: Luca, 28

Luca had made some money mistakes when he was in his late teens and early 20s. He didn't have strong money role modelling when he was growing up, so he made mistakes hard and fast. We implemented some strategies and started moving forward.

However, building up Luca's confidence was a very slow process. He had what he considered a major slip-up and had to start the self-belief process all over again. From an outside perspective, the slip-up was fairly minor, and I had expected it (you can't undo six years of money habits in six months), but from Luca's perspective, he was proving what he believed to be true in himself. Challenging those negative thoughts is an ongoing process rather than a problem that should be 'solved'.

Trauma won't go away, but it can be tempered

We can heal trauma to some extent, but it usually leaves scars in the form of a trauma response. For example, every time we stumble, negative responses will come rushing back, such as 'I knew this wasn't going to work' or 'I'm never going to fix this'. But every time we pick ourselves up, dust ourselves off and try again, we start reprogramming our faith in ourselves, which in turn starts working, just like Vitamin E cream on scars, softening them and hopefully reducing some inflammation, even if we'll have the scar for life.

It's important to acknowledge and explore our trauma experiences because they help us understand why technical skills and confidence might be harder or take longer for us to develop than for others.

Gyros

Our childhood informs a lot of our habits around money – good and bad.

Allow yourself grace when you make mistakes and identify that they were impacted by trauma.

Trauma throughout life can be triggered again and again, but we can work to reduce it.

Reflective questions

What are some of my core childhood memories about money?

What are some of my core adult memories about money?

Do I understand how they are playing out in the present, or does that need more exploration?

Are these habits from isolated events or from conditioning over time?

Are these core memories self-inflicted, or have they come from external feedback?

Part 2

External factors that influence our money

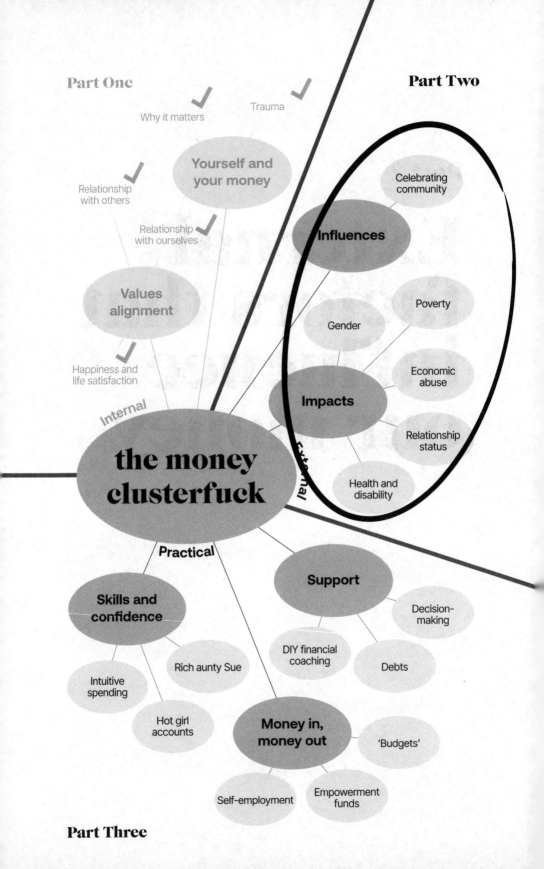

Most money books, including this one, cover behavioural changes, self-implementation strategies and personal development. Of course, this is very positive, very uplifting. Some books will also touch on external factors that affect money, such as inflation, how the market affects grocery prices and things you'd consider to be an important part of financial literacy.

These things are undeniably important to know, but as I said at the start, this book is different. I want to get stuck into factors on an individual level before anyone starts thinking about big economic systems.

It's important to touch on the many things that go unsaid in typical guides to money. There are a lot of external factors that impact our relationship to money, access to money and skills with money – factors you might never have thought about, such as gender, poverty, economic abuse, relationship status and health/disability.

If you've come this far, you likely fit into one of three types of readers:

1. You're reading this book but haven't seen anything that's at the root of *your* money issues. However, external things have happened to you that you know have played a part. If so, this is the section for you. I've also included resources at the end of the book to help you work on areas that you feel need it.
2. You're loving the book so far and can't wait to tell people about it and start implementing strategies. You know a lot of what has been going on for you is internal 'you' stuff, but this book has shown you how it might not be the case for other people. That will only continue in this section. Part of the work is broadening our lenses and making sure we're doing the least amount of harm to others who may have different roadblocks to us.

We can't heal other people's money trauma, but we all have a responsibility to educate ourselves and avoid making it worse.

3. You understand what we've discussed so far but wonder why so many people are inexplicably 'bad' with their money and unable to implement what you consider to be simple strategies and solutions. You get frustrated at family members and friends who go through the same problems and perhaps find yourself judging people worse off than you. These are pretty common responses, especially if you haven't been exposed to or made aware of the many external factors that may play a part in personal finance. No judgement here – we don't know what we don't know. However, I hope this chapter helps you understand that it's more complex than people making bad choices, and that you can empathise with people you may have previously criticised.

Regardless of which type you are, you'll find something valuable in this section. Let's crack on.

Chapter 7

A primer on financial integrity

Financial integrity is having awareness, empathy and patience for the way external factors influence both practical and behavioural money experiences. It's consistently coming back to a place of non-judgement, towards ourselves and others, when it comes to money decisions, and working honestly towards understanding and improving. It's also essential to applying the knowledge you got from Part 1 to a real-world context.

Cultural competence and safety

Australia is one of the most culturally diverse countries in the world. Not only do we have the oldest continuing culture, but we also have people living here who identify with over 270 different ancestries. People from different cultures do their money differently. They have different challenges and powerful strengths. Cultural influences shape our relationship with money, and having a basic awareness of these influences provides a space of inclusion and celebration when talking about money with friends from other cultures. It also helps us examine our own cultural biases and habits around money (as a non-religious white Australian woman, my money hang-ups are likely to be different to an Indian-Australian man, for example).

The concept of cultural competence was historically used in healthcare and is a person's ability to understand and support people from different social and cultural backgrounds. Cultural safety is looking beyond individuals to the systems and power imbalances that can affect a person's health and other outcomes. Cultural competence and cultural safety are practices, rather than things we 'achieve'.

This part of the book gives us the opportunity to deepen our understanding of how other cultures interact with money, get inspired and become aware of the different challenges they might face, both individually and at a social level through examples. While I've included some variations of how this looks for people with different cultural identities, it's not comprehensive. But to understand these stories and experiences, we need to talk about privilege first.

Financial privilege isn't just your parents buying you a car

Privilege has become a very touchy subject, especially with the rise of privilege awareness, call-outs and accountability in the age of social media. While fully exploring and interrogating privilege at an individual and social level would fill its own book, we can do a quick overview of how it applies to money and money conversations. Again, this isn't designed to be comprehensive by any means, more of a focused primer.

Side note: It's not uncommon to feel defensive about privilege, and it's good to lean into that if you feel uncomfortable. This overview is a focused call to awareness, rather than a criticism of your circumstances.

What is privilege in a social context?

The privilege I'm talking about relates to the social mechanism of inequity. Privilege is an advantage or a combination of advantages that people have because of non-merit reasons – upbringing, gender, health or body autonomy, skin colour, background, access to wealth or education. Privilege helps put people in social (or work or other) positions because of these advantages rather than merit alone. More importantly, it limits people with merit but less privilege from achieving what they deserve.

Privilege (and a lack thereof) can be intersectional, a term famously discussed by Kimberlé Crenshaw in her 1989 paper 'Demarginalizing the Intersection of Race and Sex: A Black Feminist Critique of Antidiscrimination Doctrine, Feminist Theory and Antiracist Politics'. In the paper, Crenshaw explores how Black women suffered from a specific discrimination that arose from an intersection of racism and sexism – meaning two types of discrimination combining to create a specific experience. She also acknowledged in her TED Talk that other socially marginalised people were being constantly challenged when it came to accessing opportunities. For example, they were dying without the public outcry that would come from similar deaths of those with more privilege.

Intersectionality as a term has taken on a life of its own, and colloquially it's used to refer to different types of personal and social factors that intersect with each other and have an impact on how a person moves through the world and the opportunities that are available to them.

What is financial privilege?

When I was researching this book, I discovered that 'financial privilege' is also 'the special right of the House of Commons to decide public taxes and public spending' in the UK. To be clear, that is not what I'm referring to. My definition of 'financial privilege' is accessibility to resources that create better opportunities for financial stability and wealth. Financial privilege can look like one or a combination of factors.

Generational wealth

The most obvious example when we think of financial privilege is generational wealth. The traditional example is having access to money from your parents, grandparents or other caregivers. It would also include having access to money from your spouse, children or other person/s you can rely on for funds – whether this is money lent with low/no interest, gifted money for a house deposit, a gifted car when you got your licence or asking someone to lend you $100 when you're short that week.

Knowledge

Having people around you who know about money is one of those things we often don't realise we have – until we meet people who don't have it. It's not just growing up with people who talk about their businesses and share portfolios, although those things definitely count. It's having people around you who know how a credit card works and the cost of not paying it off, who plan for bills coming in rather than scrambling for the amount when they arrive, who understand what a mortgage is and how it works, and who know how to shop around for a deal.

People who aren't as knowledgeable about these things are not unintelligent or reckless – they just haven't been around people with that knowledge. Having people around them who know this stuff, especially in their circle of influence, means that even if a person doesn't know exactly what to do themselves, they have access to trusted advice about where to go, what to learn or whom to speak to.

Encouragement

If you grow up in an environment where there is limited knowledge about money, any attempt to change, 'take risks' or do anything differently will likely be met with fear rather than encouragement. That's not a criticism of people who react with fear. A lack of exposure means our understanding is often shaped by horror stories from the media or friends of friends.

If you grow up in an environment where people have experience with similar risks or understand what you are risking or not risking, you're going to feel more confident having a go. Of course, confidence and risk-taking are shaped by many other things as well.

Backup

If you have people who support you and are financially well off, it often changes the risks and money decisions you're willing to take, usually because, either consciously or subconsciously, you know they'll bail you out if you really mess up. Sometimes you never have to test that theory because if your backup is loaded with knowledge and encouragement, you are more likely to have success, whether that's with a savings goal, business idea, buying some kind of investment or what jobs you apply for. Even having someone who goes guarantor on your mortgage is a huge form of backup that isn't available to a lot of people.

Accessibility

Not only is this about the people around us but also the things around us. Some schools have financial literacy classes, others do basic financial literacy as part of economics and some don't do it at all. Chances are there are more money books in a city library than there are in a small town library – if they have a library! Almost 800,000 people in Australia don't have access to the internet. If you're the first person in your family or friend group to be looking into financial literacy, money management or growing wealth, how do you work out what the legitimate sources are? Again, it's finding out where to start – and having people around you who can answer those questions is a game changer.

Community

This one overlaps with accessibility. Do you live in a city, regional town or remote area? Who are your school friends or colleagues? What do they talk about when it comes to money? What are their behaviours like?

Another important factor that fits into community, as well as the other categories, is stability. If your family or community is impacted by strict gender roles, domestic violence or poverty, how might that shape your knowledge and experience compared to someone who grew up in an environment where none of those things were factors?

It can often be harder as we get older because we become aware of everything we're supposed to know or do, and the thought of asking or trying to wade our way through information we 'should have known years ago' can fill us with a combination of dread and shame.

Health

Some people have chronic health conditions, disabilities or medical trauma – all of which come with ongoing cost impacts. Health privilege can also mean being able to access specialists when you need them, and resolving health concerns or potential concerns quickly and/or without debt.

The intersectional impact

Financial privilege also intersects with other privileges – race, gender, being able-bodied, language, contacts, education, stability and housing. All of these factors impact our ability to get jobs (especially the jobs we want), access investments or wealth, or even be taken seriously.

Everyone's running their own race, but some people have years of training, better shoes, are well-hydrated and have plenty of people cheering them on from the sidelines.

Case study: Ellie, 40, and Jazz, 32

Ellie and Jazz came to financial coaching to reconcile their different approaches to money. Ellie was thrifty, always on the lookout for a bargain and had strong views on having lots of savings. Jazz was a more liberal spender, paid much less attention when shopping and was keen to buy a house.

Through a combination of solo and joint sessions, we teased out that Ellie grew up in a family that didn't have a lot of money and didn't talk about money. Ellie was the first in the family to go to university and had to buy books second-hand. High school economics didn't cover money basics, and Ellie's family rented.

In contrast, Jazz grew up in a middle-class household, where everything on the shopping list got bought. While money wasn't openly talked about, there was always money for excursions and Jazz got a family loan for a car. Jazz's parents owned their own home with a mortgage, and Jazz was familiar with how borrowing and mortgages worked.

Both Ellie and Jazz had strengths, and it was about drawing those out while helping them see why the other had such different attitudes towards money.

A quick note on bias

When we talk about bias in human nature, relationships and interactions, it refers to the uneven treatment or consideration that we give to certain people or types of people because of differences, including some I mentioned earlier. Bias can be conscious or unconscious.

Conscious bias is knowingly making decisions, assumptions or judgements about people because of who they are. For example, '[These people] are bad drivers' or '[These people] are always rude'.

Unconscious bias is trickier. If we could identify it in ourselves, it wouldn't be unconscious. In 2022, Dr Mladen Adamovic from King's College London and Professor Andreas Leibbrandt from the Department of Economics at Monash Business School did a study on resumes for leadership job applications. They found that resumes with Anglo-sounding names were far more likely to get an interview or call back. One that I discovered in myself recently was being surprised when a female pilot boarded a plane. I realised I was always looking for a male pilot because that's what I'd always seen.

Bias is tricky and dirty because not only does it stop us from waiting until we know a person and/or what they can do before making assumptions about them, but it also stops other people from accessing opportunities, information or connections they fully deserve because someone has been biased against them.

What are we supposed to do with all of this information? First, interrogate your privileges. I'll provide some recommended resources at the end of the book. Second, prioritise voices that have less privilege in the category you're interrogating as that is the best way to learn and be challenged.

When it comes to financial privilege, though, I'll leave you with one recommended strategy: the Peanut Butter and Jelly (PB&J) Test. It stands for 'Privilege, Bias and Jealousy Test'.

It's super simple and allows us all to do a quick test when we're talking to other people (in this case, about money, but I don't see why it wouldn't translate to other things) to make sure our conversations are inclusive, safe, fun and genuine.

Privilege is an inescapable part of our social framework. By keeping this in mind and running through your PB&J Test during your conversations about money (and other conversations if that's a helpful mechanism), we can all have money conversations that are compassionate, inclusive and safe.

When you're engaging in a conversation with other people, especially those you don't know well, and *especially* if you're talking about money, ask yourself if you've done your PB&J.

Privilege (peanut)

- Have I reminded myself of the things I've had access to and the opportunities they've given me?
- Am I staying open to the fact that this person may have had less or a different set of privileges that may impact what we're talking about in this conversation?

Bias (butter)

- Have I made any assumptions about this person because of what I can see or have been told?
- What am I thinking without really knowing them or their circumstances yet?

Jealousy (jelly)

- Is there something about this person that might be making me defensive or jealous, such as them having more access to resources, more stability growing up or more privilege in ways that make it hard for me to connect with them?

How to deal with it

If the PB&J Test brings up things for you during the conversation, there are a couple of things you can try:

- **Acknowledge the feeling:** Identify: 'I'm feeling embarrassed/shocked/bitter/upset by this.' Once you know what you're feeling, you can decide if you want to process that feeling later or just let it pass through. If you feel comfortable, you could convey it to the person: 'Wow, I'm really embarrassed that I didn't know that about you.'
- **Ask questions:** This is all about comparing notes. 'What was that experience like for you?' 'What have you struggled with on your journey?' 'What have you been learning about, and where from?' These questions can go either way. If you feel like you might have more privilege, you can ask these to get a better understanding of the other person. And if you feel like the other person has had more privilege than you, ask questions to test your theory (maybe you've read them wrong), or to get a better understanding if they are the kind of person you might be able to learn from.

Cheeseburger and fries

(takeaways) from Chapter 7

Financial integrity is essential for conversations about money with your people – family members and/or friends.

_____

Financial privilege is intersectional and comes from many different things. Being aware of them will help you connect better with others.

_____

Practise empathy and curiosity when discussing money (and everything else) with others.

_____

Use the PB&J Test in conversation to make sure you're keeping yourself and others emotionally safe.

Reflective questions

What financial privilege have I experienced in my life?

What financial privilege have other people had that I haven't had access to?

What biases am I already aware of?

What biases do I experience?

When have I felt jealous in money conversations? Why?

What's the best way for me to deal with things that come up when I do the PB&J Test?

Chapter 8

External influences on our money

CONTENT WARNING

This chapter will discuss poverty, social security, having disability, the NDIS, economic abuse, being single, chronic health conditions and grief, as well as specific lived experiences, including coercive control and physical violence.

Many external factors influence our money. In this chapter, I discuss many of them, shaped by the real-life experiences of friends, clients, colleagues and Instagram followers. I am forever grateful to the people who have contributed to these chapters. Some of these stories came from interviews and some from written questions, so each one is different. Most of the people who contributed were well outside their comfort zone. I hope you treasure their insights as much as I do.

Poverty

Poverty falls into two different categories: generational poverty and situational poverty. Generational poverty is long-term poverty that extends into the next generation. For example, when a child is born into poverty, they go without enough food, which can affect their health and education. These children also often grow up impacted by low financial literacy. Other opportunities, such as career and economic opportunities, are also impacted by their home environment and influences. If you are modelling off adults around you who don't have enough and are continually accessing high-interest debt or living in a feast-or-famine environment, it's extremely difficult to break that cycle.

A lot of people experiencing generational poverty make money decisions that seem totally bizarre to people on the outside. But, as I mentioned in Chapter Five about scarcity, the brain is sometimes so full of competing priorities screaming for attention that there is simply limited capacity to make good decisions. It may look like inefficient food spending, getting a pet when there isn't enough to feed the family or other financial behaviours.

Situational poverty is what most of us would think of as financial hardship. It might be short-term, due to a job loss, a death in the family or a temporary injury. It could be due to an astronomical increase in rent that doesn't leave enough for everything else, or a permanent injury that changes a person's ability to work.

It can also be when a person overcommits, whether that's the Europe trip that went on a credit card and never got paid off, or having too many personal loans and credit cards and getting in a cycle where you need another one to help manage the repayments on the old one.

Regardless of what type of poverty someone is experiencing, the important thing to remember is that they've operated within a framework they thought they could control, with the knowledge they had at the time. Of course, not everyone understands or appreciates this.

Misconceptions of social security

Let's deal with the 'dole bludger' myth right here and now. The vast majority of people who are on Centrelink wish they didn't have to be. In a 2023 survey by the Australian Council of Social Services,

73% of respondents said they were eating less or skipping meals, with the same percentage cutting back on heating or cooling their homes. Harrowingly, 98% said that the low rate of income support harmed their mental health and 93% said it harmed their physical health. Finally, 94% of people renting privately were in rental stress, paying more than 30% of their income on rent.

This becomes a vicious cycle because the person on JobSeeker is so busy trying to find ways to make their money last that they struggle to find the time and mental space to submit thorough work applications. It's counterintuitive to give people so little because they may not have enough petrol to get to the interview, or they're too stressed trying to make ends meet to put their best foot forward in the interview. While the Disability Support Pension is a slightly higher amount, it still has a huge impact on a person's autonomy and quality of life, as shown by Jude's story.

Jude

Who are you, and what external factors or perspectives bring you to this conversation about money?

I am 56 years old. I never thought that I would be in a situation where my only source of income was the Disability Support Pension, that I would live in public housing or that I would be an NDIS participant.

As a young adult, I had been financially independent and had already started saving for a home deposit. I had travelled overseas twice, experienced food and cultures so different from my own, and spent hours in art galleries seeing the world and history from hundreds of unique perspectives. I was experiencing the opera, symphonies and plays at the Opera House. The world was opening up and showed so many possibilities.

I was between jobs and thought that being unemployed was simply going to be short-term. I was very mistaken. Becoming aware that I had acquired a complex psychiatric disability at a very young age had profound effects. Financially, my experiences were no longer dictated by my own skills, abilities and earning potential.

My interactions were now constrained by difficult choices made to balance an income that is officially below the poverty line.

What do you wish people could understand about accessing the Centrelink/NDIS/social security system from a money perspective?

That, upon entry into the social security system, I became a number and would be treated as such in every interaction.

Life on the Disability Support Pension involves real and difficult choices. Do I only have the heater on for one or two hours during the coldest part of the day in the middle of winter, or should I wrap myself up in a blanket so that I can reduce the costs and be able to pay the bill when it comes? After saving for an air conditioner, at what point during the 40-degree day should I put it on because I can't afford to have it for more than a few hours? I can't remember when I last had red meat, went to a movie, went out for dinner or simply did something because I wanted to.

I live in public housing, where nothing ever gets fixed. Here, I am also a number. However, I consider myself lucky because without it I would be homeless. I have no capacity to afford a private rental and any thought of owning my own home disappeared a very long time ago.

Being a number in public housing means there is no concept of providing reasonable adjustment or assistance to navigate the system, despite having a disability. After abuse and long-term physical and psychological trauma as a child, my home has become the only safe place that I can remember. I need assistance to be able to participate in home inspections. People entering is painful, confusing and overwhelming, and inspectors threaten me with a forced entry when I can't let them, a stranger, inside. I've been left a cowering mess behind a locked door that I couldn't open in full panic attack for hours afterwards, not being able to move and knowing that no one is willing to listen to me. It is shameful, belittling and erodes all confidence because I know that it will happen again.

As an NDIS participant, I am yet again a number. My life is better because I have NDIS funding to have access to supports that meet my needs. I can now access regular psychological support and have made improvements, developed goals and am implementing steps to achieve them. With funding, I can utilise a support worker to help access the community, develop avenues to be included in social activities and have financial assistance for my assistance animal.

The dark side of the NDIS is that people who do not know you or have the necessary skills or training determine your quality of life. I am basically a passive accomplice to their decisions. Additionally, these supports can be removed at a second's notice in a new funding plan and I would be left without the vital assistance that I need. It is also very difficult to acknowledge that people are only spending time with you because they are paid to do so. It is even harder to know that once the money runs out, they will not be there. There is nothing like being treated like a cash cow.

Have you noticed your money habits have changed over time as you've been able to advocate for your rights?
I have been to the Administrative Appeals Tribunal (AAT) to secure vital supports twice since becoming an NDIS participant. This 'security' is fleeting because it only applies to the plan before the AAT and there is no guarantee that they will be included again in future plans. I was unable to secure Legal Aid assistance due to the sheer number of people undertaking the same process, and the National Disability Insurance Agency lawyers and barrister made me feel like I am nothing. Strangely, their tactics had an unintended consequence. It made me angry and I fought back with facts and the legislation. Despite the traumatic and confronting moments, it fuelled something that led to enrolling in the Bachelor of Laws.

I don't know if this experience changed my money habits or not. I do think that choosing to have NDIS self-managed funding status has allowed me to source supports that meet my unique needs and have flexibility in how they are delivered. There is a sense of self-empowerment that I manage these supports and have whole-heartedly rejected the assumption that having a disability means that I am not capable of doing this myself. I choose to not allow my disability to define me because having a disability means that there are things I cannot do, some things I can't do well and others that I do well. I think this makes me the same as everyone else, not different.

What is the hardest lesson you've learned or had to learn about money as you've navigated the Centrelink/NDIS/social security system?
I am an inconvenience and nothing more than a number. When circumstances forced me to engage with government departments for financial assistance and disability support, I didn't truly appreciate how my life would change or how my capacity to choose what and how I do something would be curtailed by a long-term limited income.

What is a money-related strength you have that you have cultivated or developed? Why?
I think a person's relationship with, and understanding of, money is influenced by whether or not you are aware that money has power. Having access to money or savings creates social, economic, environmental and life opportunities. Having money can also quickly lead to immense debt, financial stress and socio-economic challenges. The knowledge of the difference is important.

Growing up, my budget was based upon the physical cash in my purse. I could only spend what I had with me. I think that the rapid growth of online banking, credit and the development of an increasingly cashless society have been accompanied by money transitioning from a physical and tangible item to one that is seen in society as simply conceptual and a number on a bank statement.

I think the easy credit purchases, accompanied by social media, fuel peoples' needs to have the latest gadget or hot item. Possessions have almost become an advertisement for social status, but having stuff doesn't define a person or make them kind, funny, naughty or likeable.

Financial security isn't about living in debt or keeping up with the Joneses. It is about understanding the difference between want and need. We will not always have everything we want in life, but if we focus on what we need first, we can change our perspectives about what is truly important and ultimately lead a more rewarding life.

Is there anything else people should know about having money conversations with someone who is working their way through the Centrelink/NDIS/social security system?
Everyone is different, but we all have so many things in common. There is immense value in treating people with respect, dignity and kindness. The financial situation that I now face was not a choice. People can end up in places not because they have made poor financial decisions, but often it is due to a variety of factors that have collided.

Economic abuse and coercive control

Economic abuse predominantly affects women, and it often occurs in intimate relationships. However, I've seen it happen parent to child, child to parent, sibling to sibling – and I'll never forget the male client who was experiencing economic abuse from his partner.

Language

People who experience violence, abuse or can label themselves and the other person differently. The most situationally safe way of describing people in relationships where there is abuse is 'person who uses violence' and 'person who has experienced violence'. They're neutral, put the person first, and in the case of the person using violence, acknowledge that a choice has been made to use violence.

Some people prefer to use the terms 'perpetrator' and 'victim'. Some prefer 'survivor'. Some use 'victim/survivor' as it respects both main preferences. Some understand their story as having an 'abuser' rather than a perpetrator. I've had clients come up with all sorts of terms, whether that's to minimise re-traumatisation or allow themselves to laugh. If you're talking to someone with lived experience or you suspect lived experience, the best advice I can give you is to pick up the language the person uses. If they use the name of the person who used violence, use their name too.

Violence

Why are economic abuse, technological abuse and emotional abuse subcategories of domestic violence? Because when we speak of violence in this context, it's not actually physical abuse. It's the violence against, or violation of, a person's human rights. That is the violence, and the different forms of abuse fall under that umbrella.

Economics versus finance or money

Money and finance are like two eyebrows – sisters rather than twins. All money is finance, but not all finance is money. When we talk about finance, this includes stuff like banking (individually and as a sector), shares and investments, just to name a few. Money is a specific part of finance that generally focuses on us as individuals, including our income, expenses, habits and relationship with money. Finance looks at systems, corporations and government funding.

Economics is like the second cousin of your two sisterly eyebrows. Economics goes beyond finance into the exchange of goods and services, markets, supply and demand, and, importantly, human behaviour.

What kind of behaviour is economic abuse?

To show how economic abuse can play out, we're going to talk about a person who uses violence, Alex, and a person experiencing violence, Blake.

Economic abuse is a deliberate, strategic use of power by Alex to deprive Blake of resources, autonomy and dignity. It goes far beyond controlling Blake's money. It extends to Blake's freedom to get a job, have social connections and get kids fed and to school.

It extends to how Blake leaves the house, and why, and when. Economic abuse is hard to explain, horrendous to get out of, and usually has far-reaching impacts, even after a person gets out.

What people think economic abuse looks like:

- Alex not giving Blake any money or making Blake account for every dollar spent.
- Alex taking out credit cards or loans in Blake's name.

What economic abuse can look like:

- Alex rationing money for Blake.
- Alex obsessively monitoring Blake's work hours and grilling Blake for being late.
- Alex keeping money from Blake, but Blake having to put all their money in a joint account.
- Alex making all the financial decisions around goals and expenses.
- Blake not having access to banking passwords.
- Alex putting all the utilities and bills in Blake's name, and sometimes not paying them to make a mess of Blake's credit score.
- Alex causing trouble at Blake's work until Blake either gets fired or leaves.
- Alex cross-checking every receipt.
- Alex tracking Blake's car.

'How did Blake let that happen?' you may think. But economic abuse doesn't start with tracking cars and changing the locks. It can start like this:

- Alex encouraging Blake to combine finances.
- Alex telling Blake how bad they are with money and that they make poor financial decisions.
- Alex helping Blake get Parenting Payment or other Centrelink payments.
- Alex pressuring Blake to not work, or work in a particular job.

So, why doesn't Blake just leave? Because Alex is making deliberate choices to deny liberty and autonomy to Blake:

- The refuges Blake could go to are full.
- Blake can't go to a bank to open an account because Alex tracks the car or the phone.
- Blake can't get cash out at the shops because Alex checks the receipts.
- Alex is charming, friendly and a great partner and/or parent in front of other people.
- Blake has no independent income.

Let's say Blake manages to get out and away from Alex. Here are some of the impacts Blake may experience even after having left:

- High-interest, short-term debt while waiting for Centrelink.
- Housing insecurity, including periods of homelessness (couch surfing, short-term accommodation, car or street sleeping).
- A destroyed credit file history.
- Being chased for debts Blake didn't sign up for.
- Risk of being found by Alex.
- Having to change kids' schools.
- Family Court.
- Having to explain the story to multiple community service organisations.
- Having no financial confidence.
- Having a brain full of problems to solve and being unable to think of the future let alone plan for it.

To show you just how complex it is, Bonnie and Renee have shared their experiences on exactly how family and domestic violence, including economic abuse and coercive control, can play out, and how it can affect financial autonomy both during and after leaving. Both Bonnie and Renee are smart, successful women, and I'm incredibly grateful that they contributed such vulnerable parts of their lives to the world.

Bonnie

Who are you, and what external factors or perspectives bring you to this conversation about money?

I am a mum of three. I've got a ten-year-old, an eight-year-old and a one-year-old. I am 34 and I'm currently doing psychology at university. I was in a domestic violence relationship for seven years, and I left four years ago now.

While you were in the relationship, what kind of access (if any) did you have to money? Did that change over time from the beginning to the end?

My experience put me back a long way. There was a lot of financial and emotional abuse. If I was 15 minutes late home from work, or if I made myself look well-presented for work, I would be accused of cheating and all sorts of things. He was tracking me, so wherever I went, he would know about it and where I had gone. Providing for my family financially was challenging before I even got the money. I didn't have access to funds, either.

Even once I left the relationship, it kept going. He had a copy of my licence, and three years later, applied for four credit cards in my name, plus a personal loan for $58,000. I found out before he accessed the money and reported it to the police, but nothing came of that.

He used Child Support as another method of financial abuse, constantly changing jobs, refusing to tell Child Support who his new employer was, underclaiming his income (saying he earned $25k when he earned over $80k). He'd get a debt and then pay it back in tiny instalments so the debt would roll over every financial year. He claimed 50/50 care of our children for a year and refused to agree to the change of care, even though I had the kids 100% of the time. I had to submit multiple statutory declarations and other evidence. In the end, he was given a massive debt and we got the backpay we were entitled to (even though he appealed it). Even doing that put us at huge risk of retaliation.

What do people not realise about the financial impacts of being in a relationship of violence and/or leaving one?

Abusers will get you in ways you can't even imagine. You can't just go to the shops, print out forms at Officeworks or go to the bank to set up a new account. There are so many little things people take for granted. It's never as simple as just leave, and even once you do leave, it's not a case of just going down to Centrelink and getting a payment. You have to tell your story so many times, to police, to Legal Aid, to the court, to Child Support, to Centrelink, to the social worker, to the school.

Everything is absolutely exhausting, from trying to change the power into your name, to the car registration – everything was a battle, and you are already exhausted from trying to keep yourself alive and safe. When people are vulnerable, never underestimate the disadvantages they are experiencing, and don't underestimate the control someone else may have over them.

Renee

Who are you, and what external factors or perspectives bring you to this conversation about money?

I am a 30-year-old law student, moving forward with my life after experiencing horrific domestic violence, for which my abuser is currently in prison.

He knew the people I lived with when I was in Melbourne, and when they moved out, they offered him their lease. We were house-mates for about three weeks before he physically abused my cat. I moved my cat to my parents and looked at leaving, but the start of COVID-19 made things complicated, and I stayed. He expressed feelings for me, and when I declined being more than housemates, he pursued relationships with a number of my girlfriends, I guess to try and provoke me. I lost those friends.

The COVID years passed, and without really knowing how or when it exactly happened, I was his girlfriend and had been for months.

While you were in the relationship, what kind of access (if any) did you have to money? Did that change over time from the beginning to the end?

He had no access to my accounts initially, but when the COVID-19 lockdowns hit, I lost my job without sufficient savings or eligibility for government assistance. When he realised I was struggling, he offered to help, which I initially declined. Things did not improve, and I found myself only eating sporadically, so I reluctantly accepted his help. We had an agreement, which was that I would do odd jobs for him in exchange for meals. I didn't realise the high cost I'd end up paying.

I found a new job and moved out, but the control had only just started. He followed me and demanded control over the money I earned. Rather than ask for the money directly, he controlled my life – dictating what I ate, where I went, how I lived. It then escalated to the point where he would demand I empty my bank account, insisting all my money belonged to him and always would. This cycle persisted for years and in four more houses. He sabotaged job opportunities and threatened to ruin me financially. Even after paying back what he claimed I owed and despite our initial agreement, he declared it insufficient, leaving me trapped in a never-ending cycle.

His threats extended beyond finances, including threats to kill me, and threats to find my family/cat and kill them too. He took things like my laptop and phone, threatening to sell them if I didn't do what he wanted. I was physically abused nightly, including being strangled.

Despite all of this, I had secured my dream job in a law firm. However, the situation at home only worsened. He faced drug possession charges and was, to my horror, running a drug empire from our house. The police raided our home and I was evicted. He took responsibility, but I was then responsible for supporting him and myself. I became homeless and living dollar to dollar. I lived in my car, studying and working, while he continued to threaten me for everything I earned.

Once I found another new place to rent, he forced his way back into the home, saying that our relationship meant we now depended on each other financially. The nightmare of manipulation, abuse and control finally reached a breaking point when he tried to kill me and was only stopped by the neighbours calling the domestic violence unit. He is currently in prison, and I am still not safe.

What do people not realise about the financial impacts of being in a relationship of violence and/or leaving one?

I was aware that I was trapped in a financially controlling relationship, but I felt paralysed. There seemed to be no escape, no place to run, and the constant onslaught of physical, emotional and coercive abuse destroyed my self-worth rapidly. Leaving this relationship felt impossible; every attempt ended in failure. His escalating drug issues and payment troubles with dangerous individuals only made it more complicated. I thought about going to the police, but he had ties to the mafia and used death threats to keep me silent.

I confided in my boss at the law firm. She tried to help, but my entry-level position meant I couldn't afford to repay her for her assistance, and I didn't want to repeat my mistake I made with my abuser.

In my experience, the financial control in an abusive relationship extends beyond just the economic aspect. It creates a pervasive sense of entrapment, where the abuser constantly seems three steps ahead. The scarcity of funds diminishes your power and control over life, and mentally you feel like you have been buried six feet under. Independence, personal thoughts and mental autonomy all slip away, and the ability to maintain any sort of healthy lifestyle is taken away. The fear of speaking out, the belief that no one can help, becomes an additional barrier when you are already suffocating.

Have you financially recovered, and if you have, how long did it take? What were the hardest things?

I have yet to achieve full financial recovery. Going into police protection prevented me from working, and the relocation to a small town has limited job opportunities, especially in the legal or many other industries. I am currently receiving Centrelink's Austudy and actively working on applying for the Victims of Crime payment in Victoria.

While Austudy is helpful, it feels degrading compared to my previous full-time employment. Saving for a fresh start has been challenging as well, especially given the economic crises from and since COVID.

I've made the decision to fully immerse myself in my legal studies and extracurricular activities through the university. This commitment allows me to focus on building my skills until a suitable and safe employment opportunity presents itself.

What do you wish people would understand better about domestic violence and how it impacts people who have it used against them?

If I can make one point, it is that domestic violence often unfolds in silence, yet the signs are present if you look closely. Individuals enduring domestic violence find it challenging to ask for help as doing so may put them at more risk of the most extreme outcomes, as it nearly did in my case.

For many years, I knew I was in trouble, but I failed to recognise that what I was enduring qualified as domestic violence. The physical, emotional, coercive and financial control I experienced is a shared reality for many others. At the time, I felt emotionally paralysed, doubting that anyone would comprehend my situation, and I struggled to find a way to explain or prove what was happening to me.

If someone is reading this in a similar position to what you were, what would you say to them?

Escaping from this situation proved challenging, as attempts to distance myself from him often resulted in setbacks. Sharing my situation with a couple of trusted individuals led to them suffering at his hands, causing me to lose their friendship. I made sure my family remained unaware. I strongly believe that if I had the financial means, my chances of escaping would have significantly improved.

To those currently facing similar circumstances, I would urge them to reach out to someone they truly trust. Share the details of what is happening, express the need for financial assistance, gather enough funds not just to leave the situation but to sustain independence, and get help from the police. Having both financial support and a solid plan in place can be crucial in breaking free from the cycle of abuse.

Being a single pringle

Managing money as a single entity has its own challenges, especially when you go from being partnered to being single – no backup, higher costs because they're not split, and you have to work harder to find people to bounce your financial goals and ideas off.

Craig

How did your relationship with money compare when you were coupled versus now you are single?
Prior to my last relationship, I was somewhat financially illiterate – paying off a mortgage but spending wildly without a budget, living week to week. My partner had a professional background in financial services and was more sensible about money matters. She generally decided how money was spent, and I would transfer money as required. Money was never really a topic of discussion.

What do you find easier or has been easier as a single pringle?
Being in full control and making my own decisions for better or worse.

What do you find has been harder?
Managing a budget is more challenging when you don't have a partner to keep you accountable. Without someone to keep you in check, resisting the temptation to exceed your food budget, such as splurging an additional $30 on premium low-fat ice cream, requires self-discipline.

What do you think people in shared-income relationships don't realise about their single friends and their money?
In shared-income arrangements, shared costs are likely divided.

Being single and living alone often means shouldering the entire financial burden. Common expenses such as rent, food, household items and streaming subscriptions are the responsibility of one person. Other scenarios, such as booking a hotel room, are also more costly for singles.

What have you achieved money-wise as a single pringle?
I've made understanding personal money a higher priority in my life. I created a budget and implemented systems to make it easier to follow that budget; for example, automated transfers into a different categorised account and using different credit cards. I've paid off all my debt by consolidating loans and making life choices to not take on additional debt for depreciating assets.

What advice would you give to a fellow single pringle who is reading this and having to manage money?
Create systems and automate as much as possible so you don't have to think about it.

People with a chronic health condition

Chronic health conditions are very common, but often out of sight. Chronic health conditions (or 'the chroni' as my friend Steph and I call it) can be not only exhausting but also unbelievably expensive, especially if you have limited or no private health cover in the public system.

Joan

Who are you, and what external factors or perspectives bring you to this conversation about money?
I am 36 years old and live fairly close to the city in a unit with my cat. I work as a public servant in public health. I have always struggled with managing my finances, and after seeing a financial counsellor, have finally managed to set up a budget and feel in control and working towards my savings goals.

In 2022, I was diagnosed with endometriosis. Prior to this, I was not aware of my condition but had a number of co-morbidities that may or may not have been related. To manage my endometriosis, I spent money on:

- private health insurance with top cover to include gynaecology and IVF
- menstruation product prescriptions and non-prescription medications
- GP visits, specialist visits with gynaecologists and fertility specialists
- pelvic physiotherapy and clinical hypnotherapy for pain management
- psychologist
- fertility preservation
- scans/diagnostics: blood tests, ultrasounds, CT scans, MRI
- TENS machine, heat packs for pain management
- laparoscopic surgery
- transport to all appointments.

What do you wish people could understand about managing your money when you have a chronic health condition/illness?
For people without chronic illnesses: I have worked in healthcare for nearly two decades (wow, I feel old!) giving me a lot of health literacy. I also have a lot of financial privilege. Despite this, it was still a massive struggle to keep up with the expenses of managing a chronic illness. Even with Medicare and private health insurance, expenses related to most chronic illnesses are high.

For people with chronic illnesses: your expenses will ebb and flow. This year post-surgery, my expenses are probably about 15% of what they previously were. While it can feel frustrating to spend money on your health, remember it is worth it because with chronic illnesses, if you don't maintain the things that keep your condition manageable, it costs a lot more when your condition worsens!

What is the hardest lesson you've learned or had to learn from managing money with a chronic health condition/illness?

You kind of don't have a choice what you have to spend your money on, and it will be harder to save when you have a chronic health condition. I learned that there will always be people worse and better off than you, and I tried to focus on being grateful to live in Australia where healthcare is among the most affordable in the world!

What is a money-related strength you have that you have cultivated or developed? Why?

I truly have yourself and Erica [financial coach] to thank for the money-related strengths I have developed.

Firstly, I was judging myself so harshly on my money habits until you [Victoria] pointed out to me that my health expenses were much, much higher than the average person. I think you said I spent more on health-related costs per month than you do in a year! So that kind of helped me to let myself 'off the hook' a bit.

You taught me about some of the reasons behind why I would binge-shop, and I realised often it was when I was feeling crappy from my health stuff. I would online shop when I was tired and sensory overloaded when really all I needed was to allow myself to rest and know it is okay if I can't 'keep up' with what I wish I could, due to health stuff.

Secondly, you taught me how to budget! By budgeting in my health, I wouldn't be caught out in the months where I had pain flares or extra diagnostics etc. as I would have money ready to go in my fund. This helped ease the financial stress and it is a habit I have continued, which has allowed me to feel prepared for whatever health stuff my future may hold.

Is there anything else people should know about having money conversations with someone who has a chronic health condition/ illness?

Just being aware that being like base level healthy is really, really expensive for someone with a chronic health condition and expenses include things you might not even include, such as hiring a cleaner, buying takeaway out of convenience as people with chronic health conditions also often don't have the energy left to do 'money-saving things' such as food prep. The financial influences of chronic health conditions are far-reaching!

Gender

Gender is an important consideration when it comes to money and financial wellbeing, and this goes beyond the gender pay gap. Max's interview is slightly different, because we talked about so many distinct areas of gender. From Max's interview, it's clear that while money maybe doesn't buy happiness, it does buy access, and access saves lives.

Max

On gender-affirming care
Money is one of the key determining factors that affects lack of access or creates a barrier to accessing gender-affirming care. You have to have private health insurance to cover the hospital stay and to cover the surgery, but there is still a huge gap. You need around $12,000 to $15,000 to pay for out-of-pocket expenses if you have top hospital cover, and if you don't have private health insurance the bill will likely run to $22,000 plus. Some people limit their time in hospital if they don't have insurance in order to afford surgery. Even just the cost of taking hormones is enough to be off-putting for some people. I am very lucky. Through running my own business, I had access to money to fund the surgery when I needed it. So I could make the appointment, and while that wasn't easy in terms of medical pathways, in terms of money, the access was available to me. That access was key and changed everything for me.

I know I am a very fortunate person to be in that position. If we're talking about intersectional access in terms of access to healthcare as well as money, there would be a lot of trans and/or non-binary people, whether that's trans and/or non-binary Aboriginal and

Torres Strait Islander people, or people from any minority or a lower socio-economic background, where they wouldn't have that fluid access – and not just in terms of money. It's the ability to access knowledgeable healthcare professionals and know about the pathways, including informed consent. Money is a certain barrier but there are also other barriers that are in some ways harder to overcome in terms of accessing gender-affirming care – where you live and your ability to navigate the system. You've got to acknowledge your privilege, even when you come from a terribly oppressed minority, and financial barriers were less of an issue for me as a 'wealthy white queer' [said with sarcasm]. I was able to access that care when I needed it and I really have to say that access to gender-affirming care saves lives.

I've now owned my own media communications business for about ten years. I made the choice to step outside academia and do media communications in a practical as well as theoretical and strategic way, and one of the decisions to do that was because things had progressed so much and people were much more accepting of LGBTQI+ people. I only really leaned into being trans in my 40s. I'm 46 now, so it's only been in the last six years or so, and to be honest, that's also when treatments have become much more accessible – you couldn't access hormones ten years ago in the same way you can now, and it can still be quite difficult depending on where you live and which GP you go to. Really, once I started my business, I earned a lot more than when I was an academic and that really helped give me access to gender-affirming care. It wouldn't have been an avenue that was so readily available on a regular academic salary with kids. There were still a lot of hidden costs. I didn't have any sick leave, working for myself, so had to have a big savings buffer to support me while I was recovering and couldn't work.

There are a lot of people who have to access gender-affirming care through self-fundraising. There are so many structural changes that are needed.

On gender and economics

Gender has informed my choices when it came to my career. I started university in the mid-90s and did honours, graduated in 2001 and went on to do a PhD. I was good at academic studies; I won a scholarship to go to Cambridge. Academia ticked a lot of boxes, but I also thought here's a career where it won't matter what I look like. Universities are by and large left-leaning and accepting of gender non-conformity and LGBTQI+ people. But it was a different time in the early 90s when I came out and I faced a degree of discrimination and physical violence on the streets and in other subtle ways – like I chose not to declare my girlfriend as my partner when she came with me to the UK when I went to Cambridge, which would have entitled her to a stipend and assistance with relocating and getting a visa. I didn't declare that because the organisation that administered my scholarship was very conservative and I made the choice not to declare that to minimise the risk of any discrimination.

On having kids

Going through IVF is expensive. It's thousands of dollars. It took my ex-partner and I a number of attempts. We tried IUI [intrauterine insemination] and then we moved to IVF and did a number of cycles before we were successful and had our first-born. We had a number of failed cycles for our second-born. My ex-partner was older than me, and I had certainly never thought about donating eggs when the doctor mentioned it. IVF was a very weird experience for me, very alienating as a non-binary person. Anything that involves biologically female reproductive stuff can be challenging and the procedures are very invasive. There are a lot of blood tests and monitoring. I did one cycle and from that, we ended up with nine embryos, two survived to blastocyst and one of those was successful and my ex-partner carried our son.

You can access IVF now as a queer couple. When we were going through the process, we weren't aware or didn't consider that Medicare would cover some of the costs. It wasn't known like it is now, so we were in the private system. We thought the only route was doing IVF through private IVF centres. But of course, when you're older, waiting for the public system can actually mean the difference between having a kid and not having a kid as well. In terms of costs, as a private patient, it does depend on your different donor arrangements, but IVF is a money-making machine. IVF as an industry makes money out of everything – every single appointment is hundreds of dollars to see a specialist, and there are lots of appointments in a cycle. You've got to pay for medication, the costs of accessing sperm, even a known donor has to go and donate somewhere that costs money. Then once you've got someone to donate, you have to keep paying the freezing costs, including if you want to keep sperm or embryos stored for the future. It really does take over your life in terms of the blood tests and the moni-toring. It preys on hope, and everyone thinks they are going to be the statistical anomaly that manages to get a baby, even when the quoted odds are very low and it might start with trying three cycles but then you end up doing ten and it adds up to be very expensive and time-consuming.

On money, gender and friendships

Money and gender are absolutely intertwined at a structural, institutional and societal level, but at an individual level, it's more about being aware of treating people and their access to money on a person-by-person basis. If you've got a whole lot of access to finances, be aware of the fact that your friends may be under huge financial pressures you aren't under, or different kinds of financial pressures, and beware of some of the frictions people face as they move through the world or the different pathways they encounter at different points of their lives. You might be under mortgage stress, but for many of your friends owning a house is unattainable and they face the pressure and instability of the rental market.

Grief

Whether it's the end of a relationship, the death of a loved one or other loss, grief can do things to our money. It could be forgetting to pay bills, not being able to eat anything except takeaway or unexpected costs such as separation or funeral expenses.

Grief is an external factor we have all gone through in our lives, whether it's impacted our money or not. Grief affects people differently and for different lengths of time.

Ashley

Dedicated to Les.

Who are you, and what external factors or perspectives bring you to this conversation about money?
I am a social worker in my late 20s living in Victoria as well as an avid planner and holiday-taker who also enjoys baking, socialising and doing fun things! I've always had very lofty goals, both financial and otherwise. My story begins with my dad's recent passing. Dad was kind-hearted, funny and generous, and had a cheeky grin that was contagious. He loved camping and his family. Prior to his death, Dad was living in a residential aged care facility and had been unwell for a period of time. He passed away in December 2023.

Before your dad got sick, what was your relationship with money like?
Pretty good! I had been able to save up by myself and put a deposit on an apartment at 26 and manage the bills and repayments solo. I have also been able to afford an overseas holiday once every two years and interstate holidays in between. I've been able to spend on things that I found enjoyable (hobbies, eating out, going to shows and concerts) occasionally, while also having a solid savings buffer that I was adding to regularly. I had a fun budget and was able to stick to that most of the time.

I certainly could have been more frugal and spent less on hobbies and what-not, but for my age, I had a pretty good relationship with money and feel like I had a good balance between spending and saving.

How did that change when your dad got sick?

I stopped spending money on going out when Dad first got sick. I didn't want to spend money on something that might take me away from him during what could be our last moments together. I had thoughts I'd go to a movie or show and would miss a call that he was about to pass. Meanwhile, I spent much more on transport as I spent more time driving to and from his aged care facility and hospital (lots of money on petrol and parking fees!) and on conveniences (such as food delivery so I could spend time with him rather than waste it on shopping for food and cooking).

There was a long period of time when we knew he was going to die quite soon but he was still with us. During this time I started doing a lot of unnecessary and unplanned online shopping. I managed it by making bargains with myself, like: 'If Dad dies I'll buy myself [insert expensive non-essential item here].' Most of these things I still have not purchased as they now have a sense of sadness attached to them.

What have things been like in terms of your relationship to money since your dad died? Were there some things you expected, or were you caught by surprise?

Since Dad's passing, I have continued to spend a lot of money and use his passing as a justification. The spending initially started with the funeral and associated costs, which were very high. This led to spending for things for myself with the justification of 'I just spent thousands on a funeral; I deserve a treat' or 'Dad would want me to spend X amount on myself since I spent $12,000 on a pretty sad party' or 'Dad would want me to have X thing.'

I am not the executor of Dad's will; however, I am aware he had some money that I will inherit along with some other family members once the will has gone through probate. I am not sure how much this will be, but estimate $10,000 to $30,000 for me. Knowing that I will be getting this money soon has also impacted my spending as I feel like anything I spend I will 'make back'.

I have also spent a lot more than I normally would on experiences and holidays. Anything I see that I think I would enjoy I will go to, without considering the cost or a budget. This comes from wanting to experience things on a 'what if I die soon' basis, the fact that Dad is no longer able to do these things and that Dad couldn't take his money with him so I may as well use it now. I have saved nothing since Dad passed because of the above factors. Any money that hasn't been earmarked for bills has gone directly on fun things.

In regard to being surprised, I was aware that funerals and the associated arrangements were expensive, but the exact figures (and how quickly payment was needed) were staggering. Everything had a price attached – even the death certificate cost money. If you didn't already have significant savings, finding the funds at an already very stressful time could be quite challenging.

The other thing that caught me by surprise was the overwhelming need I felt to buy the staff at the nursing home presents on the day Dad passed. I didn't feel that I could do anything else unless I completed this task. I spent $110 on chocolate, $46 on gift baskets and cards, and then $40 on tissues that had Bulldogs AFL team logos on them because, at the time, this seemed incredibly important.

What would you tell people about the financial impacts that come from experiencing grief or loss?

Firstly, the emotional impact of grief can have a direct impact on your finances, whether that's spending for convenience or for comfort or for a multitude of other reasons. It can also have an impact on your thinking. You do things without thinking, including buying things you may not have purchased if you were in a different, more everyday frame of mind. Managing my finances at this point in time was in the 'too-hard basket'. There were so many other things that needed to be attended to. Managing my money was the least of my worries.

Secondly, you often need time to grieve, process things and complete associated administrative tasks – informing friends and family, funeral planning, packing up a person's belongings, contacting Centrelink to cancel their payments, ceasing lease agreements or aged care agreements. This often requires time off work, which for some people means no income and potentially even endangering their position at their workplace. I needed eight days off as lots of these things can only be done during business hours. I also found it difficult to focus on a to-do list when I was incredibly sad, so things took longer than if I were in the right state of mind.

Thirdly, funerals are very expensive! While we knew Dad was sick and would pass one day, it can be hard to save for something when you don't know the exact amount you need to be saving for. I have never had to plan a funeral before, so it was hard to have a frame of reference. Beyond the funeral, there are also extravagant costs associated with burials.

Have you financially recovered, and if you have, how long did it take? What were the hardest things? If not, do you feel like you will, or has something changed permanently?
I haven't financially recovered. Even if I hadn't started spending on activities and holidays, I still wouldn't have been able to save back the amount spent on the funeral. This is even with having a pretty modest funeral.

I imagine I will continue to spend on the fun things/activities in life due to the stark reminder that life is short. I think my fun budget will remain larger than it has been previously. However, I also know I will need to funnel some money to my savings for my future and financial goals. Very recently, I have spent more time considering what is important for my financial future. I think as time passes and the grief, in some ways, seems more bearable, these things will change.

What do you wish people would understand better about grief and how it impacts people?

Everyone feels grief completely differently and there's no right or wrong way to grieve. It is important to continue to check in on yourself and your feelings and access support and help if you feel like you need to.

Anticipatory grief is also very real when you know someone is unwell and can feel different to the grief you feel following their passing.

If someone is reading this in a similar position to what you were in, what would you say to them?

Even though it's really hard right now, you will get through this. Feel your feelings and make sure you're being kind to yourself. The way you manage your money can change if you work at it. Also, even if the funeral booklet makes the pies sound super fancy, they'll be from the supermarket freezer (we saw the packaging) and not at all worth the exorbitant cost.

What these stories tell us

I hope you found those stories as valuable as I did. They go to show that as much as we can work on ourselves and our practical skills when it comes to money, our progress, strengths and strategies will all be shaped by the external impacts we've had to manage. It's important to have empathy for ourselves and others when it comes to our external money impacts, whether we're recovering from them, working around them or challenging them.

Banh mi

So many things contribute to money problems, and many of them are outside your control.

_____

It's important to recognise these external factors and have compassion for yourself and other people affected by them.

_____

Financial abuse (and other types of abuse) can happen in many ways, often without you realising. Try to reach out to someone you trust if you think you may be experiencing abuse.

 # Reflective questions

What external factors have contributed to your money behaviours or relationships?

Are there any external factors currently affecting your ability to 'keep up' with or achieve financial goals in the way you want to? If there is self-criticism, can you balance those feelings with self-compassion?

Chapter 9

Celebrating the joy of community

If you found the previous chapter heavy reading, don't worry. This chapter is exactly like its heading – a celebration of how different communities do money differently. The brilliant, sassy and funny contributors in this chapter speak about their experiences of community, rather than speaking on behalf of, or for, their respective communities as a whole.

A Larrakia/Wadjigan perspective

Tobiasz Millar – Larrakia/Wadjigan teacher, model, actor, community development advocate, icon, dog daddy.

What's something money-related that you love about your community?
Something that I love about the Indigenous community is that if you're doing it tough, you know you can count on other mob who have more or less than you to help out and give to you if they have it spare. The Indigenous community knows what it is to struggle and they live it every day. So in the times you are not struggling, you help out where you can.

They are great at supporting you through community crowdfunding or sharing bank details to receive payments. I love this about our community and our people. Even though we have less, during different times we might have more. If I'm in a 'more' period, I'll help out if I can.

What's something you know you do differently about money through the positive influences of your community?
I'm very lucky to be in the job and position I am in terms of my salary. So I know I am able to squirrel more into savings than most. I've recently just made my first investment and will see how that goes.

What do you wish people would do better when it comes to talking about money with people in your community?
I think what is important, first, is that vulnerability doesn't always look the same for every Aboriginal or Torres Strait Islander person. And just like anybody, that shouldn't be painted with a broad brush. At the end of the day, everyone's just a human being who might want to save money or want to manage their money better, or become more financially aware and navigate different financial spaces that we have been excluded from for generations.

Secondly, people, companies and systems who are interacting with Aboriginal and Torres Strait Islander people need to understand that many First Nations people don't come from generational wealth, and often don't trust the systems that help people manage and grow their money.

A lot of systems and knowledge have been gatekept from First Nations people, either deliberately or through ignorance by those people and systems that have built them. Even outside of banking and finance, it's so many things – it's when you're accessing healthcare, schooling and education, it's constantly wondering if these systems and the people running them are going to have my best interests at heart, and if I'm going to get the support I need. Are they going to be empathetic, are they going to understand the cultural burdens that I have to carry and the cultural obligations that I have?

For example, all the terminology and the language when it comes to banking, whether it's applying for loans and, you know, what a car loan looks like, or what a home loan looks like. What the fees are and what the wording means. It's not accessible if you are not already familiar with the systems – and that knowledge often comes from family and friends, or the safety of being able to ask questions without judgement. Even things like understanding how cash advances work or how you can access the money in advance and then pay it back with extra fees. That type of arrangement is totally alien to many Aboriginal and Torres Strait Islander people.

What is the biggest challenge that you have found when it comes to managing money?
I never thought I'd own a house. My parents didn't own a house until they were in their 50s and, you know, that was like such a far-fetched pipe dream for me. I didn't come from generational wealth and like I said, a lot of Aboriginal and Torres Strait Islander people don't. And it's not generational wealth like being left a huge amount of money and three houses. It's more just like, you know, having people to help you out every now and again, every fortnight, every month, you know, having parents or family to reach out to be like, 'Hey, Mum and Dad, can you just sling me 100 bucks because I'm short this week.'

Even the mortgage process and applying for a loan was a really vulnerable experience for me. I lost my mum in 2013, and have a strange relationship with my dad. So as I was going through university and then starting work as a teacher and moving into a permanent role, I was saving to get a mortgage and had been for a few years. But when I went to my bank, I didn't have the minimum deposit and the deposit they were looking for was like $60,000 to $80,000, and while I had some of that and a stable permanent job, I didn't have the whole amount. It was exhausting trying to understand what I was being asked to provide and why. There were so many barriers and so many things I was expected to do but just didn't have knowledge of. Even things in the language the bank was using like 'lendee' and 'lender' versus 'mortgagee' and 'mortgagor'. There were so many points where I almost gave up, but

I was like 'No, we've got to keep pushing and do this because we can't break those cycles if we don't keep pushing to overcome the financial trauma that I've had and experienced in the past.' In the end, I was able to start my mortgage with a government-supported lender, Keystart, and transition to a bank a few years later, and have since been able to refinance and renovate my place as well, which has been awesome.

An Islamic perspective

Mastura Koelmeyer – associate advisor in financial planning, fashion icon, money and mindset coach, mother.

What's something about money that people in your community do that you love?
I love that people in my community give to charity as it forms part of the foundation of their faith – that is, Islam. Those who have the means are required to give 2.5% of their wealth to the poor. According to the World Bank in 2016, the annual charity pool from Muslims is estimated to be up to US$1 trillion a year. Just imagining the impact this amount of money can have on those in need is something that I love about my community when it comes to money.

What's something you know you do differently about money through the influences of your community?
Values play an incredibly important role when it comes to how we approach life. I know I manage my money differently through my Islamic values and principles of Islamic finance. Something that is an integral part of Islamic finance is avoiding interest, as it is exploitative and doesn't ensure equity in exchange. Unfortunately, there are not many options in Australia for people of my community to avoid interest at this present time. However, I believe there are people from my community working hard to open the first Islamic ADI (authorised deposit-taking institution) to meet the needs of the community. I have tried to request my bank turn off any

interest-earning on my accounts, although this is not something my current bank can do and so I manage this on my own. Personally, any money I currently earn on savings I do not keep. I have set up an automatic transfer of any interest I earn on my savings to transfer into an account that is dedicated to funds I donate to charity.

What do you wish people would do better when it comes to talking about money with people in your community?
I wish people would be more open to speaking to others about money and not gatekeep. I feel as though we don't talk about money enough. Parents should teach their children about money and the importance of spending, saving and investing; it should also be taught in schools. Among many cultures, it is considered rude or taboo to speak about money, but I think we need to be talking about money to understand it better. Breaking down unhelpful limiting beliefs surrounding money can also be a result of talking about it. Financial education is especially important for Indigenous peoples, Black people and other people of colour. By talking about money, we increase our understanding of it and learn how to manage it, while developing a positive relationship with money so we can build generational wealth. When we talk about money, we give permission for others to do so as well.

A Nigerian perspective

Ada A – mother, wife, badass government officer, cash enthusiast.

Who are you, and what external factors or perspectives bring you to this conversation about money?
My name is Ada A, and I am a Nigerian. Nigeria is the most populated Black country in the world, with over 200 million people. I came to Australia in 2017 with my hubby who came to study. We had our son in 2018. I am currently working as an HR officer in a government department in Tasmania.

What's something about money that people in your family/community do that you love?

Nigerians typically use cash a lot. For example, we have a system known as Ajo/Susu, where a group of people contribute a certain amount into a pool and someone carries [receives] the total amount each month until everyone has carried.

Or another Susu system is contributing for the whole year. Then in December, the whole amount is shared equally or used to purchase wholesale food items for the community to share and consume during Christmas season as prices of food items usually skyrocket during the Christmas season.

We buy our cars with cash and build our houses with cash. I know building a house in Australia with cash would be impossible except maybe if I win lottery.

It is very common for Nigerians to build houses in stages; when the money ends we stop. We then gather more money and continue building again. It is very common to see a lot of uncompleted buildings there.

What's something you know you do differently about money through the influences of your family/community?

Example: I needed to change my car. I saved for it for almost three years while driving an old car model. I paid cash for my Toyota RAV4 2018 model. A lot of people thought I was crazy to pay about $30,000 in cash for a car when I could have taken a car loan. But Nigerian influence could not justify taking a car loan, especially for an object that would not appreciate in value. I sleep better at night knowing I don't have any car debt.

I typically shop only once a week or once a fortnight. We typically don't waste food.

What is the biggest challenge that you have found as part of your family/community when it comes to managing money?

Black tax. You are expected to support extended family financially. Cousins, friends, siblings have the expectation that since you are outside the country and earning in dollars, you should be able to give them money. Sometimes it leads to entitlement mentality and financial pressure. Children are expected to take care of aged parents financially and vice versa.

What do you wish people would do better when it comes to talking about money with people from your family/community/background?
Don't assume every Nigerian is a fraudster. We work very hard for our money and at times we just like to enjoy our money too. Nigerians like to show their wealth (think luxury items) and throw lavish parties too.

What has been the most challenging?
Lack of support and childcare. As first-generation immigrants, you work so hard that sometimes it affects family time. Having no support. A couple, most times, work opposite shifts to be able to afford the necessities of life and rarely spend quality time together.

An Egyptian-Palestinian perspective

Madonna Salem – psychologist, romantasy (romance-fantasy) obsessive, generosity queen.

Who are you, and what external factors or perspectives bring you to this conversation about money?
My name is Madonna. I'm a psychologist by day, avid bookworm by night. I'm Egyptian-Palestinian, born in Egypt, and I migrated to Australia at age seven.

What's something about money people in your community do that you love?
My culture is very family oriented, always caring and looking after one another. My community is also generous, and I love the time and effort they put into supporting those in need around them through charitable organisations.

What's something you know you do differently about money through the influences of your community?

For me, education and my environment played a big factor. I worked previously in the emergency relief sector – learning how personal and external disasters can easily impact my finances was something I took note of. Through conversations with clients and colleagues, I was more aware of my money choices and always attempted to limit my food wastage.

What is the biggest challenge that you have found as part of your community when it comes to managing money?

People want to be respected and valued and often that is associated with 'having' more money or a higher status. As a result, projection of wealth and appearance can be a challenge. People tend to spend more than what they have to keep up with appearances. This leads to further debt and shame/guilt.

What do you wish people would do better when it comes to talking about money with people in your community?

Accepting and respecting people as they are would contribute to less shame/guilt and debt. More people would be likely to spend within their limits.

How do things compare to your husband and his community?

My husband and I come from the same community. For us this means our values are aligned with one another. When we consider spending, we often look at better value and the long-term benefits of the product rather than something more affordable and likely to break in a short time.

A Chinese perspective

Rosy – dentist, mythology lover, mum to Toffee, aunty to Pebbles, Robin and Steve, future children's book author.

Who are you, and what external factors or perspectives bring you to this conversation about money?

I am the eldest of three daughters in a fourth-generation Chinese family. I was raised in a middle socio-economic status family in Singapore, and we moved to Melbourne in 2009 to be closer to my dad's family. On both sides of the family, my grandparents didn't come from money but raised their children to believe in the importance of education and self-sufficiency. As a result, my parents, aunts and uncles all did very well for themselves and they passed these traits down to us (all my cousins, sisters and I finished university). Growing up, my parents made sure my sisters and I were comfortable but also worked to instil a very healthy scarcity/ starvation mindset in us.

What's something about money that people in your family/ community do that you love?

Filial piety – being respectful and taking care of your family, particularly one's elders. This is a concept that is highly espoused in Chinese culture – we're taught about it from day one in school. I was lucky that I had a family who were willing and able to help me financially through university, and I made it a priority to repay that investment. I consider the day I bought my parents a new car one of the proudest moments in my life.

What's something you know you do differently about money through the influences of your family/community?

The importance of saving and self-sufficiency. I have my parents' scarcity mindset to thank for this. Growing up, I was always envious looking at friends who had the latest and newest. I'd envy my friends going on overseas holidays, eating out all the time and wearing branded fashion and wonder if I wasn't doing something right and whether I was missing out. It wasn't until I met my ex-partner when I realised that a lot of people may have been living beyond their means. Or that they'd just had different priorities – which was okay.

I think I was definitely very sheltered about money growing up. My parents were supportive of me getting a job, but from a place of supporting my career, rather than the financial component. The most important thing was education, to get good grades, to get a well-paying job, to take care of yourself and your family and not rely on your parents indefinitely. But I remember Dad having the 'want vs need' talk with us very young. So when I started working, the first thing I'd always do on pay day was to put money away.

Knowing the difference between a want and a need really hit home for me when I started working part-time at university. Looking back now, I knew my parents could have afforded it – but now understand why, and am thankful that they held back and didn't.

What is the biggest challenge that you have found as part of your family/community when it comes to managing money?
That money can still be such an elusive and stigmatised topic, and such a status symbol. It's all fun and games when you watch your dad and uncles argue over who wants to handle the bill (or find imaginative ways to sneak the money that Grandma gives you back into her purse), but after a while it gets embarrassing. We all joke that Chinese weddings all tend to be more for the couple's parents to one-up each other. It's tradition to have weddings be big and grand (it's supposed to bring good fortune); however, in this economy, I can't help but feel like it would be less exhausting if we just eloped.

As a consequence of being raised with a scarcity mindset, I would also feel quite guilty whenever I spent money on pleasure or experiences, e.g. coffee, facials, buying lunch. (Dad took the whole 'avocado and latte/brunch being responsible for the housing crisis' message completely the wrong way, so that didn't help.) With time, this guilt relaxed, but then I'd also find myself being paranoid about whether or not spending in certain ways constituted lifestyle creep.

What do you wish people would do better when it comes to talking about money with people from your family/community/ background?
Talking more comfortably and openly about it, matter-of-factly, acknowledging the emotional component that comes with it as – just that. That it's okay to *not* want to put on a show to impress others, but also accepting that it's an expression of love.

Having your own conversations

If you want to talk about money with people who are from a different culture or community, here are some guiding principles:

- Are they from a different community or culture, or are you making an assumption?
- Focus on the person. Ask 'How do you do [thing]?' rather than 'How do you do [thing] in your culture?' People don't owe us lessons about their culture, especially when it's easy to google it. Uninvited questions about culture can come across as asking for unpaid labour. It can also bring up trauma for the other person if they have a colonial, political and/or generational history with money.
- Do you know the person well enough to ask them about their money/culture? Some people (regardless of community or culture) consider it rude to ask. A better approach, if you want to have more money conversations, could be to ask them for their opinion on a strategy, plan or money-related topic that you're working on yourself. Over time, this can lead to organic discussions about money differences.
- Respect boundaries and read the room. If the person says they don't want to answer a question or engage in a discussion, respect that boundary. If a person is looking or sounding uncomfortable, either drop it or ask them if they want to talk about something else.

Vegetarian nachos

(takeaways) from Chapter 9

Cultural attitudes and traditions can greatly affect our relationship with money. This can be good, bad or neutral, but it helps to understand them.

———————————

Focus on 'reading the room' when it comes to asking other people about their money and experiences, especially if they're from a different cultural background to you.

 # Reflective questions

How is your culture similar to or different from the cultures reflected in the stories above?

Consider how much your culture has influenced your relationship with money. Has it influenced any of your core experiences?

What have you learned that you didn't know before?

Have these stories challenged any of your biases?

How can you include diverse voices as you continue to learn?

Practical tools and support to improve our money

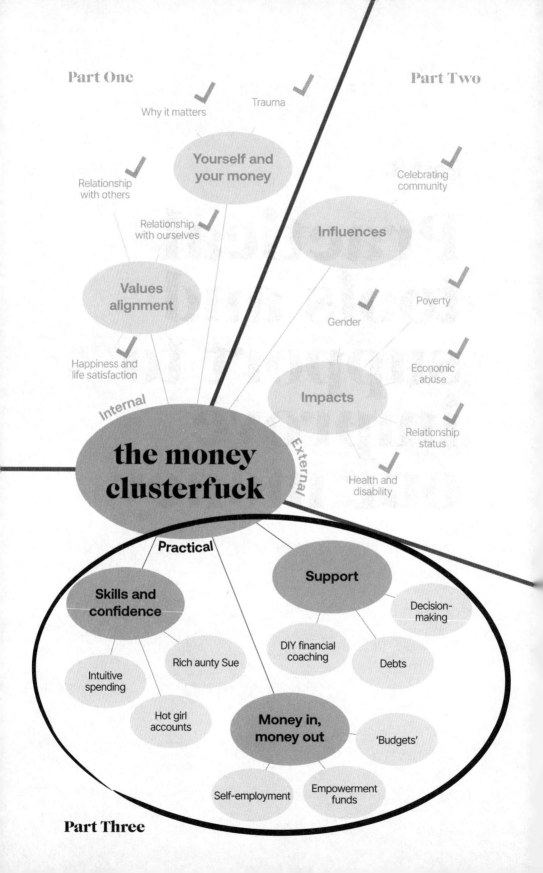

We've tackled more than half of our clusterfuck. Just look at our updated map and all those ticks. We're on the home stretch and heading into our practical skills – budgeting, account structures and paying down debt, as well as money as a business owner, empowerment funds and what on earth superannuation actually is. There are other bonus chapters as well. This section is jam-packed, and full of the strangest metaphors yet. Butter your crumpets, it's time to bite into the goods.

Chapter 10

Can we stop talking about diets in money books, please?

CONTENT WARNING

This chapter discusses eating disorders (not behaviours) and other potentially triggering topics such as fatphobia, 'healthy eating' and related icks. If you're currently experiencing an active eating disorder, any treatment needs to be supported by a psychologist. This chapter is not medical advice.

I've spoken on podcasts and in my 'A Year of Shame' talk about having an eating disorder and the struggles and shame that have come with trying to recover from it. I've been in recovery for over four years now, but being hyper-tuned into that stuff means that I really notice how much money books talk about dieting. They love to talk about how spending and saving is like dieting and 'healthy eating' and how you need long-term discipline to manage your money like you 'manage' your weight. And it's total bullshit. Absolute hot nonsense.

But what I do find interesting is how the social misconceptions about dieting and weight have a lot of similarities with the misconceptions about saving and spending. At a social level, most people believe that individuals control their weight. Somehow, we are happy to believe that some people can be naturally skinny but some people can't be naturally fat. There are so many things that contribute to a person's weight. Genetics, socio-economic status, chronic health conditions and health management, trauma, access to food, and factors just like we talked about in the lived experience chapters.

There's only so long a person can control themselves before life gets in the way or the brain takes over. We all want to feel like we have control over our lives and ourselves, but let me ask you this question: how often has controlling your food/money allowed you to avoid thinking about life events or emotions that are outside of your control?

Many of us have swung between these two extremes and fallen off the wagon more than once. If strict dieting and budgeting worked, we'd only have to do it once, right? Except we don't, because for many people, that's the only way of thinking we know. Thankfully, there's another option. You might have heard of it – intuitive eating.

Intuitive eating is a set of principles researched and designed by Evelyn Tribole and Elyse Resch, both dieticians and qualified medical professionals. It's a method of rebuilding your relationship with food and your body. It's not a diet; it's a set of principles that helps you re-learn to eat based on your natural hunger and fullness signals – without shame. Basically, intuitive eating principles help you get back to 'normal eating'.

Renowned dietitian and therapist Ellyn Satter summarises 'normal eating' as the following*:

- 'Eating competence', which is going to the table hungry and eating until you are satisfied.
- Choosing food you enjoy and eating it until you get enough, not just stopping because you think you should.

---

*   Copyright © 2021 Ellyn Satter. Published at www.EllynSatterInstitute.org
Written in 1983 and updated in 2021 based on Eating Competence research.

- Giving some thought to your food selection so you eat nutritious food, but not being so wary and restrictive that you miss out on enjoyable food.
- Giving yourself permission to eat because you are happy, sad or bored, or just because it feels good.
- Having mostly three meals a day, or four, or five, or choosing to munch along the way.
- Leaving some cookies on the plate because you know you can have some again tomorrow, or eating more now because they taste so wonderful.
- Overeating at times, feeling stuffed and uncomfortable, or undereating at times and wishing you had more.
- Trusting your body to make up for your mistakes in eating.
- Giving food time and attention, but keeping its place as only one important area of your life.
- Being flexible and responding to your hunger, schedule, proximity to food and feelings.

Normal eating is what we would do if we hadn't been programmed by capitalism, diet culture and patriarchy to 'control' ourselves. If we apply this concept to money, normal spending is what we would do if we hadn't been programmed by capitalism, spend culture and beauty standards to look for deals and make sure everyone knows how well we're doing. Instead, we'd be financially independent at an individual and social level.

Case study: Harriet, 38

Harriet came to financial coaching because she couldn't go to Target without buying something for herself, even when she didn't really want or need it, and she had a 'situationship' with Afterpay.

Harriet was tightly controlled in the rest of her life – a strict gym schedule, working two jobs and finishing her master's. She simply couldn't understand why she couldn't also get her money under control. She and her husband both earned good money and their mortgage was up-to-date. They just couldn't save consistently. Harriet loved buying new gym gear and nice things for her kids, but would feel terrible after doing it because she was dipping into their savings. Any joy she felt from buying was quickly lost.

A diet culture solution would have been to implement new methods of restricting, making it harder to spend. We chucked that right in the bin. Instead, we set up an 'intuitive spending' strategy, where there was plenty of money for spending – no guilt and no need for Afterpay. We massively reduced her savings in the short-term and focused on paying off the Afterpay.

Harriet took to this strategy like a duck to water. When there was no binge-shame cycle with her spending, she needed way less. Harriet had her Afterpay paid off in a month, and in the next five months, fell back in love with what money could do. She gradually reduced what she felt she needed (but it still felt generous), she and her husband both changed job roles and started earning more, and before she knew it, she'd paid for an overseas holiday in cash and was saving for a pool.

Giving up on restriction and allowing for flexible, guilt-free spending literally changed the trajectory of Harriet's life.

Here's what 'normal money' looks like:

- Spending on the things that leave you satisfied.
- Choosing to spend money on what you like, not what other people think you should spend it on.
- Giving thought and money to your expenses so your needs are taken care of, but not having every dollar so rigorously accounted for that you have no room to breathe.
- Giving yourself permission to spend money when you are happy, sad or bored, or simply because you want to – without this being the only strategy in your toolbox.
- Saving for big things, or spending often on small things.
- Leaving some money in your spending account, knowing

it will be there when you want it, or spending it all because there's something you really want to buy.

- Overspending at times, and feeling guilty and overcommitted.
- Walking away from something and regretting it.
- Getting it just right.
- Trusting your budgeting system to have your back.
- Allowing money to take up some of your time and energy, but not letting it consume your life.
- Being flexible and adapting to your goals, situation and needs.

When we work through your account set-up, budgeting method, money goals and all the important things that go with them, 'normal money' is the goal, not 'perfect money'. Here are some examples of how disordered eating recovery and disordered money recovery look similar, both in habit and joy.

Eating disorder recovery looks like:	Money recovery looks like:
Eating a pie and chips at the footy and only thinking about how warm the pie is.	Being able to go out for a spontaneous meal without feeling guilty about your budget.
Saying no to ice cream because you don't feel like it and know you can have it any time. Feeling no sense of loss.	Not buying the discounted pants because you know you don't need them. Feeling no sense of loss.
Being able to concentrate on your dinner companion because you don't have to do mental gymnastics about what you're allowing yourself to eat.	Being able to concentrate on your dinner companion because you don't have to do mental gymnastics about where the money's coming from.
Being able to obsess about and then take breaks from food simply because you've gone too hard on it.	Being able to obsess about goals or strategies and then taking a break when you realise you've gone a bit overboard.

Eating disorder recovery looks like:	Money recovery looks like:
Being able to try people's homemade food.	Having the budget to try new things.
Eating less on some days and more on others.	Spending more on some days and less on others.
Stopping after two glasses of wine because your body asks you to and you're not blowing anything.	Leaving your shopping cart for a while or taking some things out because you're not doing 'just one more haul'.
Resting.	Saving.
Sauce. On. Everything. If you want.	Coffee. Every. Day. If you want.

It's okay to grieve who you used to be

It doesn't matter how many years' worth of recovery work I do. I still have periods when I miss being thinner and I miss thoughtless spending. Even though I know I'm much better at processing my feelings, embracing not being in control, and having intention and flexibility in the way I eat and spend, I still miss the thrill of losing more weight, eating less or buying four pairs of shoes on sale.

But what I miss is the thrill of spending rather than the things themselves. There's nothing quite like the thrill of dropping dollars on things I don't need. I could budget for and go back to any of those things, but once the thrill of spending is gone, I'm not going to like myself more than I did before. In the same way that controlling my food doesn't bring me peace, spending for the sake of spending doesn't bring me peace either.

So, from me to you – it's normal to grieve how you used to be with money, even if that was bad for you. It's normal to still have days where you re-engage in the behaviours from the past that have done their best to protect you. Twenty years of having a poor relationship with money won't be healed in three months, and it's not reasonable to expect this from ourselves. Acknowledging that there will be grief and progress is really important in the next few chapters. Focus on normal money, not perfect money.

Supreme pizza and garlic bread

(takeaways) from Chapter 10

Managing our money can look very similar to our difficulties with managing food – and strictly restricting either of them doesn't work.

Aim for 'normal' money, not 'perfect' money. Long-term change has to be sustainable and feel good.

Focus on small, achievable wins.

It's okay to miss the days when you were spending recklessly, even if you know it was bad. After all, it's fun to spend money. But it's more fun to know you can do it without endangering your bank account.

Reflective questions

How do I manage my money, especially spending money? Am I restrictive, intuitive or somewhere inbetween?

Choose one or two normal money principles and practise them for a few weeks. Keep what works and try others when they don't.

What does 'normal money' look like for you?

What kinds of things will indicate that you're moving towards money recovery?

What are some habits you want to improve but will probably still miss when it comes to money?

How have you nailed 'money recovery' before? How can you do more of that? (If nothing comes to mind, choose one behaviour and see if you can fake your way into it. For example, forcing yourself to leave your shopping cart overnight. While it may not feel intuitive or normal to start with, you'll get used to it.)

Chapter 11

How to be your own financial coach

A lot of money books talk about your 'money story' – the life story that has influenced your money habits. In my opinion, the influence of the past is less a money story and more a witch's cauldron: the kind of thing that bubbles away in the background, causes weird effects, has more ingredients than we can ever hope to work out and often gets stirred up in the middle of the night.

In this chapter, we're going to do a deep dive into the cauldron to understand what your personal money poison is made up of, and then we're going to make an antidote. We'll talk about how to examine your money decisions without judgement, taking into consideration trauma impacts, physiological factors and general life bullshit getting in the way.

'But Victoria,' you might say, 'I just want to manage my budget better. We've already talked about external factors!' I love the enthusiasm and that you've been paying attention, but before we can get to the practical side of things, it's time to apply everything you've learned. Once you explore why things aren't working out for you, process the money (or life) behaviours you don't like and understand the patterns you *do* like, you'll be able to replicate them – and become your own financial coach.

The secret to being a good financial coach

Being your own financial coach is about shifting the dial from regret and self-resentment about your money choices to empathy and curiosity. I am not exaggerating when I tell you I have witnessed clients changing their lives, simply by understanding themselves and their past, and not being so fucking hard on themselves.

Please note: you don't have to identify every ingredient in your cauldron to make progress, and you don't need to deep dive into your subconscious every time you spend money. However, when you're feeling bad – whether that's confused, judgemental, regretful, disappointed or frustrated – about your money progress or money decisions, being able to come back to your self-coaching framework will allow you to assess what happened and move on. The secret to being a good financial coach is to never be shocked, and to always look for the link that triggered the behaviour.

My favourite questions to ask

The first question I ask clients is: 'Why do you think that happened?' If there's one thing I've learned from being a financial coach, it's this: assessing why something happened and then moving on from it is the most effective way of improving it or limiting the chances of it happening again. Beating yourself up and holding onto something with anger or guilt doesn't allow the wound to heal.

This question works whether you're trying to understand a habit, tendency, particular event or response. You can change the question to 'Why do you think that happens?' if it's an ongoing situation.

On the surface, you can ask why something happens in the short-term to explore competing things that may be impacting your decisions or habits. For example, you may miss your payments because you haven't automated them, not because you don't have the money.

You can also ask about the long-term reasoning behind things, including the deeper, older stuff that you might have forgotten (or tried to forget), such as a financially unstable childhood. Sometimes, the short and long-term will intersect and overlap; present stress can often trigger old hurts or long-term issues, like turning up the heat of your cauldron and letting it boil. That bubbling water brings up all sorts of things that have sunk to the bottom.

Case study: Carl, 53

Carl came to financial counselling because he was about to lose his house to the bank. He had a complicated set of personal circumstances, but we managed to work through them and do an income and expenses sheet with a payment plan proposal for the bank, which was accepted. But Carl kept making late payments, or missing payments, which meant the bank would call me.

When I explored with Carl why he didn't have enough to make the payments, it turned out that he was really stressed about his eldest daughter, who was having some personal issues, and custody conflict with his younger daughter. How did this play out? He had to take time off work and was smoking more. The result? A reduction in income and an increase in expenses meant home loan payments were being delayed or missed. Of course, Carl was disappointed and frustrated that he wasn't making his payments, but when we looked at *why* that was happening, we could work around it. Having someone look at the why, and acknowledge that the outcome makes sense in the situation, means carrying way less of that emotional impact around.

Carl and I spoke to the bank and we tried something else, which worked for a while. What Carl really needed to do was sell his property, but he wasn't quite ready to accept that and wanted to try other solutions first.

Don't limit yourself to the negatives

This chapter is focused more on when we have 'bad' money

behaviours. But it can also be helpful to use 'why' questions for good ones. If you have money (or life) habits that are really bloody good, or you notice you react in a positive way to a situation, ask yourself why you think that happens and start adding some nice smells to your cauldron. You'll be amazed (and sometimes frustrated) to find out how much you learn about yourself when you start asking yourself this question.

Whenever I'm having these 'why' conversations with myself, I have them in the second person. I pretend someone else is asking me rather than me asking myself. Why? Because this allows me to put some distance between myself and my thoughts, letting me moderate some of the self-judgement and gently challenge some of my assumptions.

Feel free to make the person who is asking 'Why do you think that happens?' someone else. It could be your grandma, it could be Yoda, it could be Oprah. I'm happy to be in your head, too, if you like.

Short-term questions

Getting to the heart of why something happened can be tricky sometimes, so you may need some prompts that fall under the question 'What other shit was happening at the time?' Here are some to start you off:

- What happened during your day/week that might be on your mind? How much room is that taking up?
- How are things at home?
- How are things at work?
- Are there any problems you're currently trying to solve?
- Are there any problems you're trying to avoid solving?
- How are your relationships with your parents/kids/partner/ other important people?
- Have you been eating enough?
- Have you been sleeping enough?
- Have you been taking or missing prescribed medications?

Remember the rock jar from Chapter 5? Imagine your money (or life) issue as a smaller rock in the jar. Maybe you have the capacity to change something right now, and maybe you don't. But you can definitely be compassionate with yourself.

Long-term questions

If the short-term questions don't bring any kind of clarity, or you're trying to dig into a behaviour or habit you can't seem to fix, you can start teasing out some of these. Go gently as once you start digging you might hit bone. Even though it can be hard, I've never had a client who didn't find it worth it. Have a think through these and see what comes up:

- What was money like for you growing up?
- What do you remember?
- What was it like as you got older?
- Did anything change over the years? Why or how?
  - » What are your parents/siblings like with money? Are they spenders or savers? Are they relaxed or stressed? Did you ever go without as a child? Do you feel like that was positive or negative?
- What is your partner like with money?
  - » What were you like with money before you met your partner? Has that changed since you've been together? Why or how? What about previous relationships? What were they like? Did you have positive experiences or negative ones? Have you always been attracted to the same type of person? Why or why not?
  - » What does someone who is 'good with money' behave like? Where does that image come from? What about you is different to that ideal?
  - » Do you feel like you've had not enough money or too much money? Why? How does that show itself in the way you act with money?
  - » When someone says 'blame it on the trauma', what do

you immediately think of as your trauma/traumas? Why?
What harm has that caused?

» What do you feel guilty about in your life? Do you feel like
you have reasonable forgiveness in yourself for that? If not,
why not? How does that play out in your life?

I'll say it again: our money habits have been built over [insert your
age here] years. Reprogramming takes time. We need to forgive
ourselves and embrace being a work in progress.

Questions to help prompt acceptance, coping and forgiveness

When you consider everything we've talked about in the list above,
does it make more sense why you might not have the best money
vibes right now? It's time to start working on your antidote. Take
the short- and long-term questions, and start looking at things
from a high level.

- If someone else told you they had all those factors in their
  life and their money habits came from that, would you judge
  them as harshly as you're judging yourself?
- Is whatever happened likely to happen again? In what
  circumstances? How can you plan for this?
- Rather than hoping you'll just 'do better' next time, is there a
  way you can budget, allocate or do something in advance so
  you have the option to do the thing without guilt? What else
  can you add to your cauldron that might temper the poison's
  effects? (How far can I stretch this metaphor? Stay tuned.)
  Do you need to write that down, so you remember these
  options when you need them?

Examples

Here a couple of client journeys where the questions above created
huge money breakthroughs.

Cerin

When Cerin breastfeeds in the middle of the night, she buys all sorts of things online to keep her awake and distracted from the tiny leech attached to her. Some things are cheap bits and bobs, and some things are more expensive. She often feels like she is having an out-of-body experience when she's doing it, and half the time can't remember what she's bought, leaving her feeling guilty and disappointed – even before the packages arrive.

Cerin realises through her questions that she's tired and sore, and more stressed than she's ever been in her life trying to keep her baby alive. So Cerin gives herself a 'baby brain' account with dedicated money in it that she can use guilt-free. Cerin also starts to practise leaving things in her shopping cart for the morning to see if she feels any differently, while still giving herself permission to buy them if she wants.

Priyana

Priyana grew up getting everything they wanted that money could buy. When their parents separated, Priyana's mum resented how much their lives had changed and constantly complained about not having enough money compared to before. The relationship between Priyana and their dad was strained after the separation and he was not emotionally available to Priyana. In contrast, Priyana's mum relied on Priyana for a huge level of emotional support after the separation.

Priyana is now incredibly focused on living on a tight budget so they are never stressed about not having enough or staying independent. They worry constantly about purchases and have ambitious savings and life goals. While they are on a good salary, they are hesitant to spend and keep lots of cash in reserve. They agonise over spending decisions, though they have noticed they often spend a lot on 'nesting' homewares and furnishings, especially after dealing with particularly full-on conversations with their mum.

Priyana realises that seeing their parents separate has contributed to keeping them tightly wound, both financially and emotionally.

They realise that the urge to spend on nesting is due to the subconscious craving for their own safe space, separate from the emotional reliance of their mum and the emotional unavailability of their dad. They realise they don't have a stereotypical caregiver relationship, and that is leaving them drained. They realise they are paranoid about becoming a similar burden to others, which is why they cling to their budget and goals.

Priyana tries a few things. They check in with themselves when looking at nesting items to see if there's a particular trigger from a conversation or interaction. They want their home to feel like a safe space so they limit invitations to people who don't reflect safety. They work on setting boundaries with their mum as well as their own emotional investment. They start considering what their goals might look like if emotional safety was less important. They realise they used to love playing hockey and decide to prioritise themselves and spend money on getting back into that.

*

These aren't the kinds of breakthroughs that usually happen in one hour, or after spending $300 on new sheets – though sometimes that can happen. But they are the kinds of breakthroughs that happen after gently, curiously asking, 'Why do you think that happened?'

This reflective work is going to shape a lot of your practical stuff. We need these questions for when we're working through a budget that isn't doing the job for some reason, or when we're spending money on a category we don't particularly value. In the meantime, keep stirring the cauldron and working on your antidotes.

No, I don't think you should quit smoking

When we make bad, recurring financial choices, asking 'Why do you think that happened?' isn't helpful. Sometimes, it's more about managing the situation. For example, when I was a new financial counsellor, I had a client tell me she smoked a pack a day.

'Okay,' I said, 'and how much are we looking at weekly?'

'$400 a week,' she said.

I remained calm and wrote the number down – and didn't tell her to stop. You might be surprised, but I never recommend quitting smoking when a person is trying to deal with their money issues. They usually have a lot of other rocks in their jar, and quitting smoking, a significant addiction, is like picking the jar up and shaking it for hours on end. Or, to use the cauldron analogy, turning the heat up to max and watching as the poison boils over.

This client knew how much she was spending on cigarettes, and if she could give it up, it would make all the difference. Most people struggling with expensive addictions and habits already know this. But it's better to work your smoking into your budget as you improve your money situation. We're trying to prevent from you quitting, lasting three days, falling off the wagon, and then linking this experience with the idea that you're bad at money.

When you are ready, you can quit smoking, or anything else you're addicted to. It will always be there as an option.

How to find a financial coach

Sometimes, all the self-work in the world doesn't quite cut it. Or sometimes you progress to a certain point, and you get stuck on something – an emotional block or money attitude you don't like and can't seem to move past – and you want to chat it through with someone.

There are a lot of financial coaches on social media, many with fancy websites, and it can be hard to find the one that's right for you. Financial coaches are like psychologists – it's totally normal if the first one or two (or three or four) aren't the right fit. It's also acceptable to not continue with a coach who doesn't feel right for you (or right for you anymore). You can even find coaches who do small group courses or self-paced courses.

If you're trying to find a financial coach to help you work through particular things, here are some tips. First, do they offer a discovery call? If so, great. Book a 15-minute chat and pay attention to the following:

- Do they have a good sense of humour? It makes a world of difference to work with someone who can laugh with you.
- Do they make you feel supported or judged? Chances are, you're already judging yourself pretty hard, and it's unhelpful to have someone else doing it too.
- Ask them for their favourite success story. Does it resonate?
- Ask them what kinds of people they work with. Does it sound like you?

If they don't offer discovery calls, consider the following:

- Do they have reviews on their website or Google that seem genuine? Some coaches will let you speak to a previous or current client (obviously, they will pick a happy one).
- Do they have any information about what kinds of people they work with on their website or socials? Can you ask them?
- What is their price point?
- How many sessions do they suggest? What's your total investment likely to be?
- If it's a course or group, is it the right fit for you, or are you just seeking out anything that might externalise the problem rather than taking the right kind of action?

At the end of the day, if a financial coach is making you feel stupid, annoying or unworthy for asking questions about their service (that you're going to pay for), they're not the coach for you. Pinky swear.

When you have time and space to be reflective, sit down and work through the questions and see what you begin to identify in yourself.

KFC family bucket

(takeaways) from Chapter 11

Practise asking yourself 'Why do you think that happened?' when things don't go well, and keep notes wherever possible. Do the same for when things do go well.

Don't make drastic life changes while also trying to improve your money habits.

When you are feeling disappointed or negative about your money choices, or you feel like you've gone backwards, sit down and run through the financial coaching questions and see if there is anything that rings a bell as to what might be your underlying 'why'.

Reflective questions

As we've covered so many questions throughout the chapter, I won't add any more here. Take a break, have a KitKat.

Chapter 12

The Gandalf Matrix

Ever find yourself popping to the shops to buy someone's gift and somehow come out with a new sweater, yet another pair of pyjamas, a serving platter that was on sale and two candles – none of which you needed? If you often think 'Why do I keep buying so much *shit*?', this chapter is for you. Being an 'intentional spender' is a trained life skill. The training involves a lot of connecting with ourselves, which can be extremely intense if it's something we've avoided.

The good news is, we've got a custom framework that blends a practical and emotional approach to spending. You don't have to use the framework for every money decision, and you won't need to use it forever. It's a training resource to help you connect your spending with your values, and save you from some money regrets.

The framework

When I was first thinking about this book, I used to set myself a goal of writing three brief points every Sunday. One particular Sunday, I was watching *The Lord of the Rings* and thinking about how Gandalf always seems to know exactly what he wants to do.

That led me to think about money and the idea of having a 'decision matrix' for spending it. Enter the Gandalf Matrix. It's designed to help you make your own decisions when you spend money. We're working to develop a sense of mindfulness about your behaviours without necessarily changing or stopping them.

Eventually, you'll know intuitively what aligns with you and what doesn't. Sometimes you'll override your better judgement and spend the money anyway, and that's okay, because we're human. But in the meantime, we can actively engage with our spending process, building on the reflections from the last chapter.

There are two matrices – one for things and one for experiences. However, if you have particular questions you need to ask yourself in the process, feel free to make each matrix your own.

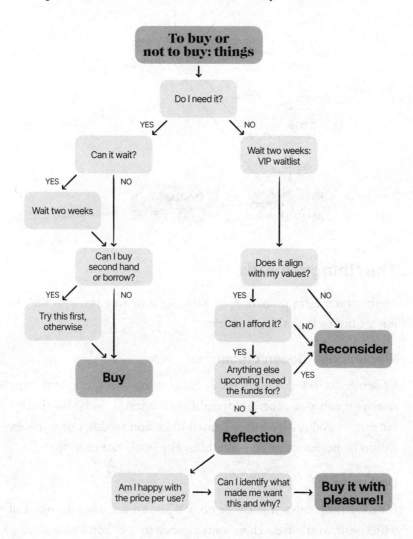

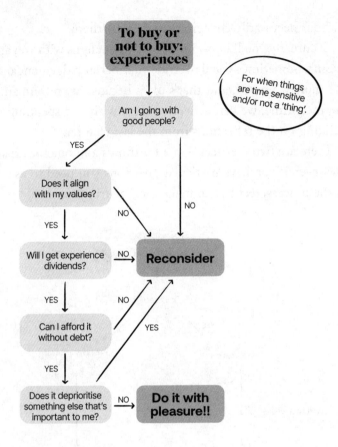

The 'things' matrix

Here's some extra guidance for working your way through the 'To buy or not to buy: things' matrix.

'Reconsider' doesn't mean no

When 'reconsider' is your result from using the framework, that doesn't mean you can't buy the thing. It's just a nudge to think a bit further about why you've landed there and whether that money would be better spent on something else you'd rather have.

Do I need it?

It's okay if the answer is yes or no. It's just an acknowledgement of which side of the flow chart you're going to use. You know in your heart if it's a need or not, and at this stage of the journey, we want to avoid lying to ourselves as much as possible.

Yes, I need it/Can it wait?

Do you need a hedge trimmer in the next month, or do you need a shower head immediately because yours has flown off?

Can you buy second-hand or borrow?

Does your neighbour already have a hedge trimmer? Can you buy a refurbished phone to replace your smashed one?

No, I don't 'need' it/Wait two weeks: the VIP waitlist

If you're thinking about something you don't need, park it in a list on your phone called the VIP (Victoria insists I be patient) waitlist. It's like an emotional cooling-off period. You'd be amazed at how many things I've added to my VIP list only to check it a couple of weeks later and realise I had completely forgotten about them.

Case study: Darcy, 66

Darcy came to financial coaching for a range of reasons, but one of them was that they would often buy things while watching late-night TV. When we worked through 'Why do you think that happens?', a lot of what came up for Darcy was feeling alone and tired at night.

So, while we worked on the emotional side, we also implemented a 'wait until the morning' logistical strategy. Darcy could put something in their shopping cart or write down the hotline for the 'must-buy-now' product. We also implemented a strategy where Darcy bought something and left it in the box for two days when it arrived – as almost everything has a 30-day 'no questions asked' return policy. These stopgaps gave Darcy the opportunity to reflect on the reason for the purchase and space to *reconsider*.

Does it align with my values?

As discussed in Chapter 4, your happiness doesn't have to look like anyone else's. It's about what's important to you when it comes to spending. Do you value beautiful things, convenience, relaxation or experiencing as much as possible? I value efficiency, so I place importance on things or services that allow me to get the most out of my time.

You may value clean, tidy spaces, so buying ski equipment for your Japan holiday and keeping it in your house for years may not align with your values. You may buy a Tinkerbell costume for a dress-up party because you value giving your kids creative freedom, and a dress-up box fits in with these values.

Can I afford it?

Do you have the cash put aside already? If not, can you save a bit longer for it or raise the money in another way? Do you have something at home, or does someone in your circle have something at home, that will make do? I used to borrow my neighbour's mixing beaters because I would only need them one or two times a year and couldn't justify buying my own.

Do I have anything coming up that I need this money for?

Check your calendar, texts and birthdays. Are you good to spend that money now?

What will my price per use likely be?

Are you going to use that massage gun every week? (By the way, I bought one, and I have *not* used it every week.) This is especially important for clothes and shoes. How many times do you think you'll use or wear them? Divide the cost of the item by that estimation. Are you comfortable with the final price per use?

Can I identify what made me feel desire for this purchase and process why I feel this way?

Is there an emotion behind the want for this item? How did you realise you wanted it? Interrogate (gently) if the want is practical or emotional, knowing you can still buy it, regardless of what conclusion you come to. Are you trying to fill a different need with a thing?

Experience matrix

Experiences have a different matrix because the questions reflect the fact that they are not things and are often time-sensitive.

Am I going with good people?

Life is too short to hang out with people you don't like. At the very least, the people you don't like need to be outweighed by a supreme number of glorious people. Better to have FOMO (fear of missing out) than EOGST (expense of going out for a shit time).

Does it align with my values?

Does this experience align with what you value in an experience? Are you going to an EDM party because all your friends are going, when you'd actually rather be at Cold Chisel?

Will I get experience dividends from it?

In his book *Die with Zero*, Bill Perkins talks about 'experience dividends' – how great memories give back to us over and over as we relive them in our future. Sure, this can be a once-in-a-lifetime event, but it can also be those soul-filling dinners with friends on a Tuesday night that you never imagined would be as special as they turned out to be.

Can I afford it without debt?

This one is pretty straightforward – make a budget assessment. We discuss this further in Chapter 15.

Does it deprioritise another goal that's important to me?

Have you got anything else on the radar that may have to be sacrificed if you go ahead with this? Is the trade-off worth it? Remember, there are no right or wrong answers.

*

Whether you use this framework or one of your own creation, having a system to 'check yourself before you wreck yourself' when it comes to spending goes a long way. If you like, make your matrix into a wallet card. The Gandalf Matrix is a scaffold you can use until your intuition builds its own process. Eventually, you'll get to the point where you rarely need it.

Storm Oreo™

(takeaways) from Chapter 12

The next few times you're about to buy something non-essential, go through the flow charts. Getting a sense of what purchases align with your values and goals will help you develop normal money habits.

Be honest with yourself during this process. If you find yourself resisting the flow chart or justifying going against it, explore why.

Remember, the aim is not to *never* spend on anything again; it's to allow you to mindfully reconsider.

Reflective questions

Like the last chapter, there have been so many questions built into the chapter that we don't need to add more here.

Chapter 13

Connect your account names with your account purpose

The age of two-account banking is over, and the age of personalised sinking funds has begun. In the people-who-talk-about-money world, these are accounts set aside for specific purposes. For a lot of people, swapping to this style of money management is a process of self-discovery and also tends to minimise that stressful 'how much can I spend today?' energy.

Of course, using personalised sinking funds won't magically sort out your money. If it were that simple, we'd all be there. However, it *will* change your relationship with money for the better. Here's what having a fun and purposeful set of accounts is going to do for you.

It makes budgeting, like, way less shit

The word 'budget' comes from the Latin word 'bulga', which means 'bag' or 'purse'. 'Budget' literally means to 'get the bag' or 'get the money'. That definition single-handedly changed my perception of the word 'budget'.

'Budget' is such a loaded term. I used to hate it – it's too restrictive. But a budget isn't a restrictive tool. It's just a plan for how you want your money to work for you, and you don't ever need to use a spreadsheet (unless you want to).

Imagine that you open your bank app and you've got this staring back at you:

- Spending
- Bills
- House deposit
- Savings
- Holiday.

Sure, it's descriptive, but it's also boring. No wonder money doesn't want to hang around in those accounts. Now imagine you open your bank app and you've got this staring back at you:

- Destiny's Child (bills, bills, bills)
- MINION MONEY LEECHES (school fees)
- Jennifer Coolidge (injections, hair, nails etc.)
- Paulette's Palace (house deposit fund)
- Fuckboi (stuff that crops up every now and again to remind you it exists)
- PUPPY LOVE (saving for a puppy)
- GMTFO (emergency fund – get me the fuck out)
- Non partirò mai (Italy trip). (Translation: I will never depart.)

Are you not entertained? Of course, there's not-fun stuff that you need your money for. But let's give some life to something so important to, well, life.

You can plan for things specific to you

You get to decide how many accounts you need. You get to decide how much goes into each one. You get to decide what they're for. You get to add or take away ones you don't want. You get to give the accounts names that inspire you, keep you focused and make you laugh.

We'll be doing the budget deep dive in Chapters 14 and 15. But for now, think about what you want to have an account for. Or, if you already have accounts for specific purposes, think about new names that don't have the equivalent energy of the Wonder White crust at the bottom of the bag.

There are plenty of examples of how creative, psychotic, personal and hilarious these can get.

Account name	Purpose
Bubble O'Bills	
Adulting	Bills, other boring life expenses etc.
Destiny's Child	
Treat yo'self	
Burn, baby, burn	Treats, spoiling yourself etc.
Bad bitch treats	
Baby, u make me crazy	
Baby got back	Baby/IVF fund
WHAT AM I DOING?	
This is going to hurt	
FFS	Emergency fund
Are you kidding?	
Lose control	A specific account for those who blow through cash when they are struggling (it happens to a lot of people and it's okay to plan for it)
Going off the fucking rails	
You made me ink	Tattoo fund
Fuckboi	Inconsistent expenses such as annual insurances, dentist, vet, car services etc.
Scarecrow (for things that 'crop' up)	

Account name	Purpose
Maddison's Mansion *Krishna's Krib* *Hinkley's Hotel*	Rental/mortgage payments (feel free to choose an alliterative name that works for you)
Sub to Cap (subscribing to capitalism)	Unplanned, spontaneous purchases, or things you can't escape spending money on
FML (fund my learning)	Education
Boujmobile *Rich mum taxi* *Madinator/Smithinator/ Kathinator (adjust to your first/last name)*	Car fund
Adventures	Fun experiences for yourself or with others
Bump and grind	Exercise/gym membership
GET ME OUT *Toodles*	Travel – country or trip-specific names are highly encouraged
Baby got bank *Rich girl/gay/they energy*	Investing
Sorry, I'm busy	Books or other hobbies
Yes to the dress	Wedding fund

My mortgage broker bestie, Jess Campbell, recommends changing these spicy account names before you go for your mortgage application or refinance. I tested mine (yours won't necessarily be the same), and if I change the name and redownload the statement, it changes the name on the statement straight away. You don't want to have to explain to your lender why you have an account called 'snitches and bitches' or something equally ridiculous.

Case study:
Matilda, 28, and Muhammad, 36

When Matilda and Muhammad came to financial coaching, they weren't doing too badly at all. Their joint goals were to pay down a few small debts, get their bills taken care of when they came in, and save for their elopement and honeymoon. Matilda also wanted money for brunch with the girls etc., while also leaving some for her sewing hobby. Muhammad just wanted some money for himself without anything specific.

So, we set up four joint accounts – debts, bills, a combined irregular expenses/emergency account and an elopement fund. We called them 'bye, debt, bye', 'couple kerfuffle', 'oh hello' and 'Norah Jones'. We gave both partners the same amount for them-selves, but Muhammad kept his in one account ('cash cow') and Matilda's was split in two ('bottomless brunch' and 'stitch in time').

The period tax(es)

Did you know that while the GST on period products was (finally) abolished in 2019, period-getters will still spend roughly $10,000 over their lifetime on period products? And that doesn't include pain management. For people who have polycystic ovary syndrome and/or endometriosis, getting their periods can mean time off work, pain management and substantially more period products – not to mention the associated costs for specialists, medication and other treatment (like Joan's story in Chapter 8).

But the period tax doesn't end there.

At the tender age of 31, and after 20 years of having my period, I unexpectedly bled through my tampon, my underwear and my work pants (that were thankfully navy). Unfortunately, the horrors hadn't finished. My girlfriend had given me applicator tampons to try (if you know you know, and if you don't, be thankful). Let me tell you, I was sweating by the time I worked it out. When I finally got back to my desk, I was like, 'I need to buy something.' A bit of emotional spending is a fine thing to have in our coping toolkit, and today was the day for it. I'd been wearing these cheap shoes for about six months and they were killing my feet every time I wore them. They were the last straw. So I went out and bought new underwear, normal bloody tampons and shoes. And let me tell you, I felt much better.

My Instagram followers also overwhelmingly say yes to spending more when they're on their period or leading up to it. Food is a big one – bleeding and being emotionally stretched is hungry work – but a lot of people also said their impulse spending is noticeably up at this time, too. Whether or not that's because hormones impact emotions, which then impact financial choices, having a period could affect your money progress.

So, if you know you're going to have financial needs during flowgate, why not have an account for it? Maybe that money is to top up your food budget, to allow for the period products and pain relief you need, or because you damn well know you will need (and, frankly, deserve) a treat. Here are some naming ideas to get you started:

- Flowgate
- It's about bloody time
- Seeing red
- FUCK
- Not pregnant
- Reset
- Chalice Palace (chalice is an ancient symbol for the womb!).

Vegan burrito

(takeaways) from Chapter 13

Start thinking about things that are important to you and that you want to have money set aside for.

_____

Start a list of the accounts you want to have. Shortlist names.

_____

Consider adding an account for period spending if you get periods.

_____

Make sure there are no issues changing the names back if you need to download statements for legal purposes, such as rental applications.

 # Reflective questions

What are some account names you're itching to use?

How do aligned account names help or not help your feelings about budgeting?

What kind of accounts do you want names for?

Chapter 14

The power of mind maps and why Excel makes me want to vomit

Something about Excel, the traditional budgeting tool of the decades, gives me the extreme ick. I've never learned to use it properly, so the extent of my skills is (=sum) and data validation. Whenever I try to make a budget in Excel, it always looks as dry as a two-week-old brisket. Enter the mind map.

Why I love a good mind map

I love a visual. If I can make something into a flow chart, mind map or other drawing, I know I'm going to understand it so much better. It's spread out. It's colourful. It's got lots of white space. My brain smiles.

When it comes to budgeting, I love a mind map because all my money is on an even playing field. I can see my essential spending, my fun spending, my goals and all my savings – and they all have an equal place. Plus, my budgeting mind maps are fun, creative and colourful – exactly what I want to reflect in my life. Add in some crazy account names and money becomes exciting, exactly as it should be.

Let me show you what I mean. This first example is a simple

budgeting mind map. I've kept the account names as their traditional representations. We'll get to the quirky names at the end.

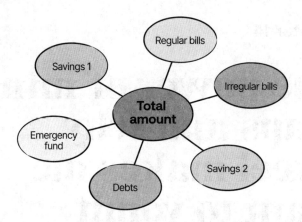

Each bubble represents a different bank account. You might end up
with a mind map that has fewer bubbles or one with more bubbles.
In the next chapter, you're going to make a stunning mind map
of your own. You can do it by hand – I recommend nice paper or
cardboard. Glitter pens are optional. You can do it on the computer.
You can do it with origami. And most importantly, you're going to
add your own account names. But before we do that, we need to
cover some preliminary steps.

Surviving vs thriving

There's a big difference between a surviving budget and a thriving
budget. If you're in the process of paying off debt, trying to manage
on Centrelink income or raising kids alone, your budget might be
very simple and very tight. That's okay. We do what we can. This
process will still empower and support you in getting the most out
of the income you have.

Case study: Penny, 45

Penny came to financial counselling because she had fallen behind on her electricity bill. She was on a Disability Support Pension and had no other income. Her surviving budget looked like this:

- Rent, electricity, water and gas – all came out via Centrepay (where Centrelink pays the funds to the creditor).
- Account 1: 'Basics' – food, medicine etc.
- Account 2: 'Treats' – this was usually $40 a fortnight.
- Account 3: 'Buffer' – this was usually $10 plus any leftover from Account 1 to build up extra money for when it was needed.

Monthly budgets – it's a no from me

If you get paid monthly and struggle to make your money last all month, put your wages into a separate account and pay yourself out of it weekly or fortnightly. You can call it the 'quarter chicken and chips' account, or the 'half chicken and chips' if you're doing it fortnightly.

I do this myself. I get paid fortnightly and put half into one of my other accounts – because I can't be trusted to make it last. I like breaking it down weekly. The thought of my poor brain doing mental gymnastics trying to remember what's coming up or what I can spend this early in the pay cycle is too much, and I'm okay with that. So, I pay myself weekly and run with my other strengths. Plus, it's such a thrill getting paid *every* Thursday.

If a monthly budget works for you, run with it. Congratulations on having the self-control of an Olympian. If you prefer a micro-managed structure and have different accounts for each category for each week, that's cool, too.

Don't pay your bank

When you create your mind map, you're going to need a few more bank accounts. This is an excellent opportunity to do an audit on the accounts you already have because there's plenty to take into consideration. Most importantly, fees. A bank charging *you* for holding *your* money – when they get to use it as well – is bin chicken behaviour. If your bank charges you monthly fees on any of your accounts, move on. You and your money are too precious to pay a monthly fee. Google 'no-fee transaction accounts'. Plenty of online banks offer it.

If you find moving overwhelming because of your direct debits and wages, do it gradually and leave your main transaction account with all that stuff until last. Focus on setting up all your new accounts as fee-free, and when you're good and angry about having paid $4 a month for the last 10 years ($480 for nothing), move all your debits over and bin your old accounts for good.

By the way, most banks that are members of the Australian Banking Association offer a basic bank account for customers who have a concession card – including a Pensioner Concession Card, Health Care Card or Commonwealth Seniors Health Card. They're designed to keep banking affordable for people on lower incomes.

Banks are also obliged to proactively monitor for customers who may be eligible for a basic bank account. So, if you're eligible for one and have been paying account fees, ask your bank to waive the last 12 months (at least) of account fees as a goodwill gesture.

These bros ain't loyal

Don't keep all your money in one bank. In the digital age, unexpected outages happen all the time, not to mention human error. I locked myself out of my entire travel account for half of my overseas trip in America. Luckily, I had my other transaction account with a different bank and just paid myself back from my travel account at the end.

The other reason you should do this is to avoid scams. Everyone thinks it will never happen to them until it does. Money spread around different banks minimises the chances of losing large amounts.

I have my FFS fund and my treats account with one bank (one card, one saver), and most of the others with a separate bank. You might like to keep your emergency fund separate if you're tempted to use it or keep it front of mind if it makes you feel safe.

It's best to wait until you've drafted your mind map to decide how many accounts you need. I prefer to have as few cards as possible, so I focus on having mostly savings accounts and only have cards for my treats and adulting accounts. If I need money from one of my other categories, I transfer it to a card account. If you prefer having four cards, go for it. It's your party, baby.

Half a chicken and peri peri chips

Draw your draft mind map. Think about what you need and why, and have some fun with the names! It's okay if your mind map changes down the track.

_____

If you get paid monthly, use your account structure to 'pay yourself' fortnightly or weekly.

_____

Audit the accounts you have. Keep any no-fee ones for now. Move (or work towards moving) away from any accounts with fees.

_____

Note down which accounts need a card and which don't.

Reflective questions

How many institutions do I currently bank with?

Does the thought of lots of bank accounts feel comforting or overwhelming?

Am I paying fees on any of my accounts?

Which accounts might I want to split across different banks?

Is my current pay structure working for me?

Chapter 15

Creating a budget you don't hate

I'd been tracking expenses for a grand total of two months when I spent $500 in one month on eating out. 'Jesus Christ,' I thought. 'Am I doing that every month?' For me, $500 in a month (for one person, with no super-fancy meals) was a lot. Thankfully, I've rarely come close to that since. Fine dining isn't high-value for me, but quality time with friends is. That month, I'd caught up with two friends who were in from out of town, a group I hadn't seen in ages and a few other catch-ups here and there. The money was worth the quality time spent. I managed the financial impact because I have a budget that I don't hate.

You're doing yourself and your money a disservice when you don't have a plan. Without one, your money will disappear, even if you don't mean it to. Having a structure where your dollars know where they are all going, whether they're reserved for fun or work, allows you to get the most return on the time you spent getting the dollars in the first place.

Account types

Here is a heads-up on the types of accounts you'll need for your budget:

- **Regular expenses:** The expenses you need to pay – housing, utilities, food, childcare and direct debits such as health/pet insurance, gym membership etc.
- **Irregular expenses:** The expenses that are irregular and often sting. Think car registration, servicing and insurance, professional registration costs, dentist, specialists, optometrist etc.
- **Treats:** Stuff that isn't essential to living but essential to happiness.
- **Debt paydowns:** This is where you take your debts from your shit list to your hit list (see Chapter 19). If you have no debt, you won't need this.
- **Emergency fund:** I use 'emergency fund' as most people are familiar with this term. However, think of it more as your ultimate empowerment fund. You can build this up for whatever you want – quitting a job, replacing your hot water unit, insurance excesses, emergency flights home etc.
- **Sinking funds:** As discussed in Chapter 13, this is a goal account for whatever you want: holidays, school fees, starting a charity, home cinema, tattoos etc. I once had a client with a knitting fund.

Let's do your money

You can do this exercise sitting down at your computer, at a desk with highlighters or in bed with your banking app. In this example, I'm working with a salary of $1500 a week for a person named Betty. It's okay if your salary is less, or more – your bubble numbers will all be different, too. We'll run with $1500 for now.

Step 1. Start with your regular and irregular costs

Let's get the basics squared away. Go through at least three months of bank transactions. At the moment, you're looking for your regular and irregular 'needs' expenses. Have them on two different lists, one for regular and one for irregular. Include what they are, how often they occur and how much they are. I recommend going back anywhere from six months to a full year to catch your irregular expenses in full, and to get a better idea of your utility costs. There can be a big variation between your summer and winter costs for these.

Case study: Pietro, 32

Pietro didn't know why his budget wasn't working. There were times when he didn't have enough in his bills account for the bills he was getting. When we audited his expenses over a longer period of time, Pietro realised he hadn't accounted for his water rates and his uptick in electricity for his air conditioning in the summer. He'd done a great job of planning but needed to go further back to capture everything and smooth it out.

Even though a mortgage is a debt, if you have one, count your repayments as a regular cost in this part rather than a debt paydown. Debt paydowns should focus on non-housing (and usually high-interest, high-stress) debt. Your notes will look something like Betty's.

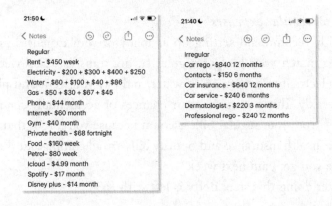

Work out what this means for your budget

Assuming you're doing your budget weekly, you need to convert these to weekly costs. For your utilities, get a full year's worth for accurate averaging.

Taking Betty's examples from above, we take the irregular expenses and convert them to an annual figure. This comes out at $3380. Divide this by 52 and you get $65 a week. Looking at Betty's regular expenses, we calculate them depending on their regularity. For her utilities, which are either bimonthly or quarterly, we add up the total yearly cost across the different amounts and then divide it by 52 weeks. The amounts that are monthly we just divide by four, and the fortnightly amounts just by two. If possible, we add a small buffer into the weekly amount to provide some coverage when things fluctuate slightly, or if we don't quite have enough in there to cover the expenses the first time around while the system is getting set up.

Total weekly cost of $801.

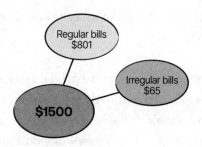

Note on regular expenses

I highly recommend setting up as many of your expenses as you can to match your budget regularity. So, transfer $23 a week to your electricity account, $6 to water, and pay your rent and phone bill weekly. This minimises your chances of accidentally spending money from your regular bills account because you forgot that your phone, health insurance and Spotify bills are all coming out the day before you get paid next week.

After doing this step, Betty is left with $634.

Step 2. Controversy

Rather than adding your debts or emergency fund next, I recommend choosing your treats fund. Let me explain why. A common problem when sticking to a budget is that we aren't giving ourselves permission to spend.

In both financial counselling and financial coaching, clients would say, 'I keep dipping into my savings/bills/expenses account and blowing it,' or 'I can't stick to the budget I set myself.' They all wanted to know how to change what they saw as a moral failing. I asked them how much money they give themselves to spend and 90% of the time they said 'None, I can't afford to be spending money on myself with these debts,' or 'Whatever's left at the end.'

In theory, that's all good. But money was getting spent anyway, and it was getting spent hard. They would have this shame-spend cycle where every time money was spent when it 'shouldn't be', they were miserable and swore to 'do better' next time.

Deprivation causes desperation. If you're starting a new system, having a healthy dose of money to spend makes it far more enjoyable, and you're more likely to succeed. So, find a way to increase the fun money as much as possible – even if it means reducing debt payments to their minimum for a while, or reducing your savings rate (especially if you were dipping into it anyway). And if you can, increase it a *lot* to start with.

Once you acknowledge the shame or despair the overspending is causing, invite it to come in and take a seat at the budgeting table. It chills out. If you get your amounts and strategy right, you'll often have money left, you'll be more relaxed about buying things for yourself and you'll end up spending less. The trick is not to force it.

If you start feeling guilty about treating yourself, remember, it's all part of the process. The more generous you are, the quicker you'll adapt to having permission to spend, and then you can tweak the budget amounts as you go.

Adding the treat fund

Most people have a rough idea of what their minimum debt

repayments are, so keep this in mind when you're choosing your amount, though you can always rejig this if you get to the end and the numbers aren't where you'd like them.

Betty knows she has roughly $150 a week in debt payments, so she's not going to give herself $600 a week. She's also got a couple of other things she wants to add. So, Betty gives herself $275 a week, because she wants to be generous, but she feels $300 is excessive.

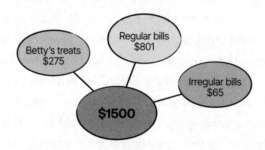

Step 3. The battle of the priorities

When it comes to emergency funds versus debt, which comes first? This is a fine balancing act. You don't want to miss payments on your debts because you're trying to build up your emergency fund, but if you have no emergency fund, the chances of having an emergency are much higher.

Wherever possible, I'd recommend making minimum payments on your debts, and then adding to your emergency fund (we'll talk about your emergency fund in detail in Chapter 17). There will be ways to increase the debt account and start your proper debt paydowns, including:

- Adding more to the debts account if there's leftover.
- Reducing the treats fund over time.
- Having extra money come in from somewhere.
- Having enough in our emergency fund that you feel safe pausing it for a while.

Conveniently, Betty has $169 in minimum debt repayments (just a little more than her estimate), leaving her with $190.

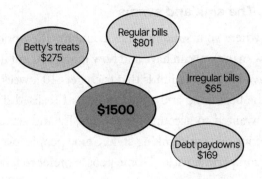

Betty doesn't have any money in her emergency fund yet, so she's going to drop $100 per week in there until she has a bit of a cushion.

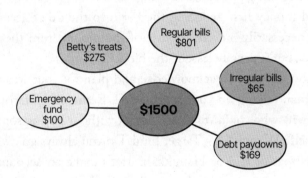

If you already have an emergency fund, or you don't have any debts, the choice is easy. You can smugly skip Step 4. But if you don't have enough left to cover all your debts, or you're only scraping by with $20 to $30 to spare, make sure you read Chapter 19 on debt paydowns. You may find it easier to pause here and get stuck into that chapter first.

Step 4. The sink and swims

Here is where your sinking funds come in. The options are endless with how many you can have and how much you put in each one. You could have ten sinking funds that each get $10 a week. I started with two in the beginning and added more as I realised there were other things I wanted to account for specifically and separately. A lot of this depends on your thinking style. Some people love to have lots of labelled compartments, and some people prefer to have just a couple.

I've had quite a few clients set up a 'going off the rails fund' because they have a mental illness or health condition that causes them to lose a lot of control when it comes to spending. This particular sinking fund acts like a stop-gap. The person prepares while things are good, so when things are bad, they go through that reserved money first, reducing the harm to the other accounts. It doesn't necessarily prevent the use of the money from their other accounts, but it usually lessens the blow.

It's always better to acknowledge and plan for your weaknesses, rather than relying on your self-control. Remember Harriet from Chapter 10, who couldn't go into Target without buying something for herself? We created a Target fund. Do you always go overboard at Christmas or Eid or Hanukkah? Let's make an account for it and save all year round. Want to invest? There are sinking funds for that, too. Your sinking funds don't all have to be goals, and they don't have to be lofty, fancy ambitions. They are whatever *you* want.

Betty decides that she's going to have two sinking funds. She's going to save for a cat and for laser eye surgery. Each fund will get $30 for now. It's not much, but she'll work on adjusting it as she goes.

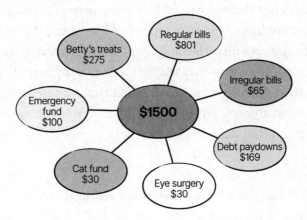

With her last $30, Betty wants to save for a trip, but because she doesn't have any savings to work with, she's going to top up her irregular expenses account for a while, just in case something is due before she's saved enough from her $65 a week.

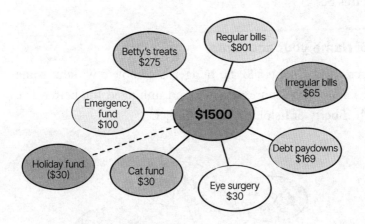

Considerations when choosing your sinking funds

What always catches you out in your money cycles? Is it council rates, school supplies (and the dreaded shoes), specialist appointments or insurance renewals? For me, it was always my licence, registration and pet insurance, so I needed to make sure that was planned for somewhere.

What do you always wish you had more money for, or always feel bad about not having money to spend on? Maybe that's flowers for yourself or your partner. Maybe it's gifts, donations or cute stationery. Maybe it's the movies – they cost a small car repayment these days. Now is the time to create space for that thing. Sometimes, clients found this an absolute joy, and other times, having the money there meant the craving went away. Either way, it's a win.

Leftovers

If you feel like you've done what you need to do on your sinking funds and still have money left over, you can:

- Top up your emergency fund.
- Top up your irregular expenses.
- Start smashing your debt down.
- Create a 'hold and wait' sinking fund until the answer finds you.
- Consider investing (see the recommended reading at the end of this book).

Step 5. Name your accounts

As discussed in Chapter 13, no budget is complete without some custom names – the more personal and unhinged the better. I've taken the liberty of helping Betty with hers.

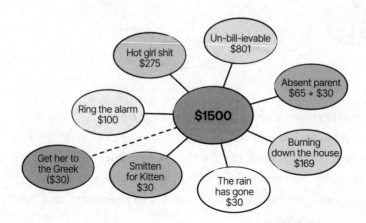

Look at this – money that is flexible, fun, practical, creative and personal. What a moment. Cheers to Betty, and cheers to you when you finish yours.

On couples

As we discussed in Chapter 5, couples should *always* have some separate money. Whether that means having a mind map that looks like this:

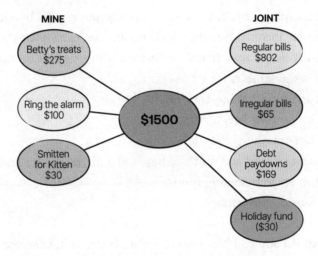

Or a mind map that looks like this:

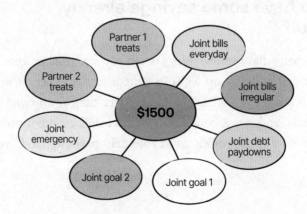

It doesn't really matter, as long as you're comfortable with how it will work. With the shit I've seen go down when couples separate, it's better when both people have a few thousand each (like a personal emergency fund, for example), but I've found that many couples don't like hearing this advice. Of course, your joint accounts must still have fantastic names. Just because you're monogamous, there's no excuse for account names that are monotonous.

On extra cash and bonuses

Avoid counting extra cash or bonuses into your regular budget if it's not regular income. But there's no reason you can't have a plan for it when it does come. If you get extra cash or regular bonuses, my advice is the same as for leftovers:

- Top up your emergency fund.
- Top up your irregular expenses.
- Start smashing your debt down.
- Create a 'hold and wait' sinking fund until the answer finds you.
- Top up your sinking funds.
- Consider investing.

You can do any combination of these. If you've taken care of the basics, you have plenty of options.

If you have some savings already, kick off

If you already have some savings when you start this process, I'd first recommend building up $500 in your irregular expenses and then build up a healthy emergency fund. After that, you might want to shift gears, and put a couple of hundred dollars into your sinking funds to start you off or kickstart your debt paydowns in Chapter 19.

Teriyaki and green tea

(takeaways) from Chapter 15

Follow in Betty's footsteps to create your own bespoke bag (budget).

_____

Include as you can and give yourself room to treat yourself.

_____

If you're sharing some finances, decide which partner model works best for you.

_____

Have a plan in place for any extra income or bonuses.

 # Reflective questions

Have I prioritised a healthy amount of spending money?

Where am I worried this budget might fall down? Why? Do I have an adjustment strategy?

How often do I want to check in with myself to see how well this is working?

Chapter 16

Tracking your expenses and the fail-fast method

Like avocado on your sub, tracking your expenses is something extra you can do at the beginning of your budgeting journey or down the line. While it's very helpful, especially if your budget bubbles keep bursting, it's not an essential feature. I'm not going to lie to you, friends. I didn't track my expenses for many, many years. I saved and used my categories for spending, so I felt like I didn't need to bother. And if I'm being completely transparent, I didn't want to know how much I was spending on what. So, if you don't want to do this, don't, especially if you want to go slow and steady in your new relationship with money.

Once I started tracking my expenses, however, things became really interesting. I started with a few categories and built it out when I noticed patterns. The app I use is called Spending Tracker. It's super basic and manual. The icon in the App Store is a brown wallet and it's also available on Google Play. It has a free version with ads. I bought the paid version for $5 after I'd used it for a few months and knew I'd be keeping it. I add my income in as well, and the app gives me an overview of what's come in and what's gone out.

Some people love apps that automatically pull all their

expenditures and pre-categorise them. That's not for me. Firstly, I'm a bit iffy about third-party access to my banking and transactions, and secondly, entering and categorising my expenses manually helps me think about how I felt spending that money on the 'One to 10, would I spend again?' scale.

One to 10, would I spend again?

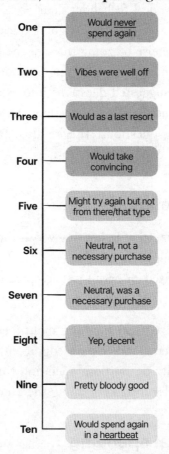

One	Would <u>never</u> spend again
Two	Vibes were well off
Three	Would as a last resort
Four	Would take convincing
Five	Might try again but not from there/that type
Six	Neutral, not a necessary purchase
Seven	Neutral, was a necessary purchase
Eight	Yep, decent
Nine	Pretty bloody good
Ten	Would spend again in a <u>heartbeat</u>

Use the scale as a super-quick reflection on your purchases. There shouldn't be any judgement involved – just curiosity. You can still do the 'would I spend again?' test even if you're not tracking your expenses; for example, you could reflect on your purchases once a week while looking through your transactions in your banking app.

I don't recommend analysing everyday purchases – you wouldn't want to invest time thinking about how you rated your petrol purchase – but reflecting on your non-essential spending is a great way to test and refine your personal spending values.

If expenses bring up any feelings for you, or you're consistently spending on a certain category that you rate below a seven, you can continue the curiosity with another great financial coaching question: 'And how do I feel about that?'

You can do this as part of your ongoing tracking, or you can do it as a standalone exercise by going through the last couple of weeks of your bank statements and reflecting on your spending.

I've split some suggested questions into essential spending and non-essential spending. These questions are companions to the financial coaching questions. They're also specific to individual purchases, not behaviours or patterns.

Essential spending

- Is this essential (that is, housing versus the gym membership you're not using)?
- Is this price fixed, or have I just accepted it for longer than I should have?

Note: You don't have to do anything about these answers immediately. It's just noticing and acknowledging, otherwise you run the risk of 'accidentally on purpose' spending three hours changing your phone provider instead of doing the exercise at hand.

Non-essential spending

- How did I feel before buying this (was there an emotional trigger)?
- How did I feel as I was buying this?
- How did I feel a few hours later?
- How did I feel the next day?

- Does what I bought still have the same shine on it as when I first bought it?

Here's how I do it

Every couple of nights, I go through my banking apps and add what I've spent to my Spending Tracker and categorise it. I currently have a lot of categories (it's what my brain likes), but you don't have to. Current categories are:

- Shopping essentials
- Shopping boujee – this is when I buy fancy bread, salads or stuff for charcuterie
- Out with friends – always a good investment
- Out alone – this helped me differentiate between eating out with people I cared about and eating out because I'm tired or grumpy
- Fuel/public transport
- Boujee bitch shit – stuff that's unnecessary and an attempt to bring me joy
- BB beauty – haircuts, laser, eyebrows and makeup all go in here so I can keep an eye on them
- Professionals – specialists such as a psychiatrist, financial advisor and dermatologist
- Car-related
- Health.

There are more, and I really go overboard, but that's how I like it. You could have 20 categories or four – whatever works for you.

Take an old-school approach: other ways you can do it

I used to keep these categories in a spreadsheet and give them a satisfaction rating (ultimate finance girlie behaviour). I quite enjoyed it, but I simply didn't have the time to keep it up. If you love a spreadsheet, though, go to town. There are some good templates on Etsy. Or you can write them manually! Some people love a good notebook and just keep a running total. As someone who regularly can't find their car keys, trying to remember a notebook is too much to ask in my case.

Some things you'll love buying; some you won't. Sometimes you'll ignore your feelings when you buy something, and sometimes you'll pretend to feel good about it. Remember: normal money, not perfect money. Whether you decide to track your expenses in detail or just do a two-week transaction review every now and again, you'll keep learning about yourself and what you actually value.

The fail-fast method

As you start working through your budget, there's a possibility it's not going to be quite right the first time. In fact, getting it perfect the first time is the exception rather than the rule. That's why we need to talk about the fail-fast method. This method is used in tech but also organisational psychology.

It's the idea of prototyping something (such as making a draft for a system or product), testing it quickly to understand where it falls down, and improving it from there. Basically, it's failing on purpose quickly to produce higher-quality success. I absolutely love it and how we can apply it to money and life. It's the concept of starting something rough and improving each time. Let's explore how it could apply.

Instead of trying to nail your budget mind map the first time – or drafting one, and when it doesn't work after three weeks, assuming you're unhelpable – you deliberately anticipate failure. The 'prototype' in this case is either doing it with a couple of accounts first or tracking your expenses to help you define your categories. Then you test, observe and redesign. This is what it might look like:

- Setting up a couple of sinking funds first.
- Manually transferring the amounts instead of automatically.

- Not cancelling your old bank accounts immediately, even if they have fees, because all your direct debits are still there.
- Having a sinking fund to anticipate things you forgot to include in the budget.
- Tracking your expenses for two to four weeks at first to see your patterns and what account structures might suit you.

Let's say you're trialling a new set of accounts. Rather than overhauling everything and setting up 40 automatic transfers, you add one account – an easy one, with a straightforward amount and minimal debits. Maybe it's your irregular expenses account. Trial that first and see if it works. If it does, great! If it doesn't, still great; it's one less thing to try. Time to tweak and try again. The failure becomes a strategic element of the success rather than the make-or-break. It's much easier to dust yourself off when you're anticipating a fall.

Case study: Keenan, 22

Keenan came to financial counselling as she couldn't make a budget work. She'd tried apps, spreadsheets and accounts. Because of Keenan's ADHD and depression, we had to be patient in finding the right option. First, we tried the mind map method with some budgeting accounts, but Keenan was still using some of her expenses money for fun stuff and leaving herself short, and then getting frustrated. So, we tried taking the money from her 'fun stuff' bubble and putting it in an envelope so it was tangible and separate.

That helped, but it still wasn't quite there. So then I had Keenan do an expenses audit in her account to see where her money was going, which took time, including going through it together to help with procrastination.

Keenan identified a couple of categories she wanted to improve now that she had visibility on how much she was spending. We also increased the amount in her spending fund generally – even though it was a squeeze for her other accounts – just to take some of the restrictions away. That didn't need to last forever, and focusing on improving a couple of categories while keeping things generous was the first thing that worked, and we built from there.

The fail-fast method can also be used for work projects or side-pieces/hustles. It's embracing failure as an expected part of the process and taking it as an opportunity to change our mindset from being bad at something to being open to continuous improvement.

So, if your first mind map doesn't work, adjust it. If a whole mind map is going to be too much, do a mini mind map with one or two extra accounts first. If the mind map is overwhelming, track your expenses first. You are capable of nailing your money. Everyone is. You just need to find your hammer.

Foot-long Italian BMT

(takeaways) from Chapter 16

Before you start putting things into place, have a plan.

Decide how long you want to try your first strategy before moving on.

Make a note of what your chosen backup plans are, and what you'll try if your first strategy doesn't work in the allocated time.

Consider a mini expenses tracking challenge. Try it for two weeks or a month, and see what you learn.

Reflective questions

How do I feel about tracking my expenses?

Would I do a casual audit every now and again, or would I do it regularly?

Is the fail-fast method a lower-pressure option for me in the budgeting/tracking process?

What would that look like for me?

Could I use the fail-fast method in other areas of my life, just to get started?

Chapter 17

Diamond rings and empowerment funds

The 'emergency fund' is referenced in every personal finance book ever written, simply because it's *so* important. But it doesn't have to be restricted to emergencies. Essentially, this is money that's deliberately stashed away for a 'just in case' moment. Different people have different opinions on what an emergency fund should be used for, but I think it should cover both strict financial emergencies – your hot water system breaking down, an insurance excess, unexpected job loss, as well as situations like leaving a toxic job/person/house. Ultimately, though, it should be used for whatever reason inspires you, and you should keep it locked and loaded with cash. I use the term 'emergency fund' because so many people are familiar with it, but I think it should actually be called an empowerment fund.

The reason I say this is because many of my clients knew an emergency fund was important, but it was 'distant important'. There were so many things that needed attention first – debts, birthdays, fixing the leaky tap. There was no urgency because an emergency hadn't occurred yet. I get it. But trust me, having an empowerment fund is a game changer. If you still need some convincing, I've got a 'choose your own adventure' for you:

- The diamond ring principle
- The touch-the-butt principle
- The FUCK YOU, LARRY principle
- The BB cream principle.

Remember, if you have to call your bank about your account or submit any forms, you might need to use these account names, so don't forget to change them back/keep this in mind as you create new accounts.

The diamond ring principle

Imagine you had a high-clarity, beautifully cut diamond ring. (If anyone is getting one for me, I prefer a brilliant round cut, but I will also take an oval. Yellow gold, please.) However, you don't have any insurance for your ring. So, every time you wear it, you're paranoid something might happen to it. You can't really enjoy it because there's always a little voice in the back of your mind that says 'what if?'

It's the same with money. Your progress, savings and developing relationship with money are like your diamond ring. Without a 'just in case' fund, there will always be an undercurrent of apprehension when you're making money decisions, especially big ones. Is it safe for me to use this money now? One singular event – such as the ring being stolen, or you running into unexpected debt – can undo all your hard work, clear out any other savings and leave you feeling crushed.

If there's one thing the universe loves, it's testing a person who is working to improve their money skills – and this test generally comes in the form of a financial emergency. Building your diamond ring insurance policy will likely feel like a tug- of war – you'll start and something will cause it to go back a bit, and you fight to pull it forward again. But fight you must, because that ring is really nice and, importantly, it's all yours.

Case study: Jack, 38

Jack had just started building up his 'just in case' fund. When I asked him how it was going, he sighed and said, 'I had $500 saved, and then I had to go to the dentist for an emergency root canal which used it all.' He paused for a moment and continued, 'But without it, I wouldn't have had the $500 and would have had to go back into debt.'

Maybe the diamond ring principle is enough to inspire you, in which case, I have some account name recommendations for your 'just in case' empowerment fund:

- Diamond ring
- The four-carat
- Insurance policy
- Bacon saver.

The touch-the-butt principle

Maybe the diamond ring principle isn't a good argument. You understand why it matters, but it's not enough to inspire you to have a dedicated go at it. Let's try the touch-the-butt principle.

If you haven't seen *Finding Nemo*, here's a recap. Nemo, a small clownfish with uneven fins, rises to the challenge in the face of his father's doubts. He swims away from the safety of his friends and school group to touch a faraway boat, which his friends believe is called a 'butt'.

'Touch-the-butt' is proving to yourself that you can make it happen, that despite past experiences, despite past attempts, you can do it. This is the sheer grit option when you create your 'just in case' fund so you can smack that butt and prove that you can save yourself financially – whether you're proving that to yourself, other people who have doubted you or both.

Here are some account name recommendations:

- NEMO
- Touch the butt
- Don't test me.

The FUCK YOU, LARRY principle

Who is Larry? Larry is your awful colleague who doesn't pull his weight, has problematic views and yet somehow is still middle management. You might have a whole unbearable workplace of Larrys you're desperate to escape, or maybe one day, Larry yells at you for something minor. Larry is also your partner who can't put their washing in the basket, but thinks you wouldn't survive without them and their 'support'. Larry might be your housemate who starts growing marijuana in your shared bathroom.

Larry is anyone who makes a large and/or important area of our lives feel like shit. Enter the FUCK YOU, LARRY (FYL) fund. The FYL fund might need to be more generous in its dollar goal than some of the other principles, but it's worth its weight in gold.

The FYL fund is created so you have money for when there is a situation that makes you go 'fuck you', 'fuck them' or 'fuck this'. Whichever it is, you have some money to back you when walking the hell away, two middle fingers up, screaming, 'FUCK YOU, LARRY!' Honestly, it's satisfying even imagining it. Here are some account name recommendations:

- FYL
- Fuck you
- Fuck this
- Fuck them
- Middle fingers up
- BYE, LARRY.

The BB cream principle

The most flexible principle of all is the BB cream principle. BB cream is 'blemish balm'. If you've never heard of this miracle cream before, it's basically a sheer, tinted cream – somewhere between a tinted moisturiser and a foundation. An empowerment fund can work much the same way as BB cream. Let's see it in action.

Smooth things over

BB cream evens out your complexion to 'smooth things over'. If you're new to your money journey, it can take a while to get your groove right. A payment will default because you forgot about it, or you need to pay a doctor's fee in full before you get the Medicare rebate. While this isn't the true nature of a traditional emergency fund, when you have a 'just in case' or 'empowerment' fund, there's a good argument for it to be available for 'growing pains'.

Hiding things you can't quite deal with yet

A bit like a nasty pimple, where just riding it out is not an option, we can use our empowerment fund as the BB cream for expenses that are unexpected and a little bumpy. For example, say you've started budgeting for your yearly expenses, only your school fees and professional registration come through together and you're $300 short in your 'irregular expenses' fund. This is where your empowerment fund steps in to cover for you.

Financial scarring

I have dermatillomania, which means I obsessively pick my skin. I'll have you know that BB cream does the *most* at covering it up. Similarly, if you've got financial scarring – maybe an old debt crops up or you have to have a root canal because you haven't had the money to go to the dentist in five years – just blend that BB cream, baby.

Not a full budget babe yet

BB cream is a gift if you need a little coverage but aren't a full makeup babe yet. In the same way, if you're not a full budget babe yet, an empowerment fund can give you just enough coverage so you can get through until you're able to add other accounts into your structure and get it how you want it. Account name recommendations are:

- BB cream
- Tinted moisturiser
- Blend and snap.

How much do I need?

You tell me. A single pringle with no kids and a permanent job is probably going to need less than a family of five where one parent is on a contract. A couple with no kids may be able, and willing, to have a big empowerment fund, whereas a single parent on Centrelink may only be able to have a small one.

If you like, you can have a short-term empowerment account goal that you sprint for, and a longer-term one that you work towards at a slower pace. Here are some guiding questions that will help you shape that amount:

- How many people/pets does the emergency fund need to cover?
- Which of the principles am I most excited about?
- How much would it take for me to feel safe to execute the principle I've chosen?
- What is reasonable for me to achieve?
- Is there anything else I can do to bulk it up faster?
- How many weeks' worth of my income would I ideally like to put aside?
- What do I want to achieve from my empowerment fund and what would it take to get there?

Getting there: the thermometer method

Now that I've convinced you that an empowerment fund is essential and can be whatever you need it to be, the next part is building it up. Break your goal amount down into increments, like temperatures on a thermometer. The key is to keep yourself sweet on the goal while you're headed there. For example, let's say you're aiming for $1000. Your thermometer might look like this:

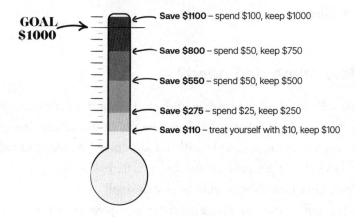

So, aim to buy yourself a reward at your thermometer marks but adjust them accordingly. If you're going to have a $100 massage at $1000, make that goal $1100 so you still have a lovely round number after your reward, and watch just how unfuckwithable you become.

Lamb korma with naan

(takeaways) from Chapter 17

Think about which empowerment fund principle resonates best with you and why.

_____

Get clear on your reason and write/draw/make a collage for you to come back to.

_____

Calculate your amount using the guidelines above.

_____

Draw or write out your thermometer after deciding how you're going to stack your rewards.

Reflective questions

What is the definition of an empowerment fund for me?

What am I going to call it?

Am I going to have one goal amount, or a sprint goal and a long goal?

How much am I aiming for?

What thermometer markers are going to keep me motivated?

Chapter 18

Budgeting when you are self-employed

I've had a lot of small business clients come through my financial counselling door over the years. As there are entire books dedicated to running a successful business, this chapter is focused just on small-business-owner budgeting, including for people with a side business or who are thinking about starting one. It covers common problem areas for clients, as well as simple tools you can use, especially in the early days when you're still getting your head around invoicing, profit and loss, balance sheets and forecasting.

This chapter may seem somewhat gloomy. I don't mean to scare you off running a business, but I've seen the devastation when running a business goes wrong. A good plan, a good team and a good appreciation for tax and superannuation go a long way in making sure your business is fun and causes the least stress possible. We'll talk about the obligations you face as a business owner and how to keep on top of them. Before we start, let's discuss the three main types of businesses.

Sole trader

A sole trader is a self-employed person who runs their own business. You have full control of your money and decisions, but you also have full responsibility for the business. The income from your sole trader business gets added to your total personal income and you pay tax on this. You are liable for the business, so if something goes wrong, the things you own personally are also at risk.

Partnership

A partnership has two or more people (or structures) involved. There are a few different types of partnerships and it's always worth getting advice from an accountant before starting one. Each partner doesn't pay tax on the total income earned, but rather, on what they make after expenses, according to their ownership portion of the partnership.

Company

A company is a different structure of business. It is legally separate from you, so it has more protection. If the company gets sued, your personal assets are (usually) not at stake. A company is more expensive to run than a sole trader business, and has different reporting requirements. Speak to your accountant to make sure you get this part right. The company pays its own rate of tax out of income, and as a director, you only pay income tax on any salary you take from the company.

There are also other structures such as trusts, charitable organisations etc. I'll leave it with you to speak to your advisor and/or accountant if you'd like to consider those options.

What to consider if you're starting a business

There are both benefits and challenges when it comes to starting your own business. I've included some key things to work through if having your own business is something you're thinking about.

Costs

These depend on what type of business you're going to start. A business with a shopfront and multiple staff has different costs to a home-based virtual business or an industry-regulated home-based business, such as mortgage broking.

If you're starting a side business to diversify your income, earn extra cash or have fun, your planning is probably going to be more lowkey (though it depends on the complexity of your product or service). The table below shows you what you need to think about when it comes to your launch planning and ongoing budget.

Premises/location	Will you be based at home, or in an office, a shop or a workshop space? Will you be subleasing? If leasing, how long is your term?
Professional costs	Do you have professional or business licensing, registration or memberships?
Insurance	Does your business need insurance? What types – professional indemnity, workers compensation, public liability, premises and vehicle?

Databases and subscriptions	Do you need accounting/invoicing software, client management software, payment software, industry-specific software etc.?
	You can often get free accounts when you have very few clients, but make sure you're happy with the costs as your client base grows.
	Tip from Bianca Bristow, OH Accounting: *Consider your scalability when adding new team members. Look at how your future choices integrate to save future you a headache. Change can be time-consuming.*
Website/socials	How are people going to find you? Do you need help setting this up?
Utilities	If you're using a physical premises, you'll need internet/phone, water, electricity and gas connected.
Banking	If you're starting a business, keep the banking separate. Your accountant will thank you later.
Support professionals	Do you need an accountant and bookkeeper? Do you need a lawyer for any contracts, agreements and terms and conditions?
Materials	Are you making something? Where are you getting your materials? Do you need trade accounts?
Cybersecurity	If you're digitally collecting sensitive information, what cybersecurity is required?

Personal borrowing

If your business is your only source of income – or you've just started your business and aren't drawing any income yet – this will impact your ability to borrow as an individual. If you need a mortgage, car loan or any other loan in your personal name within two years of starting your business, speak to a broker and accountant first so you can come up with a strategy in advance.

Treat your business like a sports team

If you love numbers and you're committed to managing your financial obligations as a business owner, that's amazing. For everyone else, hire professionals. If you (or your professionals) don't know the numbers in your business, you're in for a bad time. I've had clients almost lose their houses as sole traders because of a series of unfortunate business management issues.

Even star players (that's you) need a support team to play at their best. They need a manager, a coach, sometimes an assistant coach, a physio – you name it. Here are some of the key support team players to consider:

- **Your coach (an accountant):** The person who helps you strategise and play by the rules. They work with you on your tax return and other reporting obligations, as well as structuring your business, tax minimisation and general business health.
- **Your assistant coach (a bookkeeper):** The person who makes sure everything is in order for the coach. They keep your business's incomings and outgoings up-to-date, reconciled and organised. Some players won't need an assistant coach or they might add one later, depending on the sport.
- **Your manager (a financial advisor):** This person is looking at your long-term career. They want to get you in a comfortable position so you can retire when you can't play the game anymore. They're looking at how your business interacts with your personal finances and goals, what your future management plan is for the business if something happens to you, and your insurance coverage if you get injured during play.

Pay your shit

The Australian Tax Office (ATO)? More like Absolutely Terrifying when Overdue. If you can't afford to pay your taxes, you can't afford to have a business. That might be the harshest sentence in the whole book. We're all obliged to pay tax, and the ATO does not take kindly to being neglected. If you're a sole trader, there are far-reaching impacts for not staying on top of your tax.

Case study: Snezana, 50

Snezana had a consulting business that she operated as a sole trader. She fell behind in her mortgage payments and a number of other debts due to health issues affecting her work. She had also fallen behind on her tax returns and business activity statements (BAS). This meant there wasn't enough income coming in and decisions had to be made. As her income was primarily from her business and she was in financial difficulty, her bank needed to see updated debts and her ongoing capacity to pay, including any outstanding tax.

As a financial counsellor, I needed her tax returns done to see what options were available in terms of payment plans, budgeting and submitting proposals to her creditors. If the situation couldn't be fixed and she needed to file for bankruptcy, her tax returns and BAS needed to be up-to-date so we could make sure she was declaring everything she owed.

Unfortunately, Snezana's business records weren't in tip-top shape and she desperately needed the help of a bookkeeper and/or accountant. But because she was struggling to pay her bills, it was a whole lot of extra stress and cost to deal with.

Just like when you get paid by an employer and the tax comes out on your behalf, the best thing you can do is accept that the government gets some of your income. Not only do you need to keep this aside, but you also need to factor it into your charge rates. If you're worth $100 per hour, is that before or after tax? I would say it's after, so your charge rate should be more like $140 per hour to account for some tax and super.

How much tax should you estimate?

This is not an easy question to answer because it depends on your business structure, earnings, other income and whether you're registered for GST. It's rarely less than 30%. Speak to your accountant or call the ATO, which also has some decent preliminary information on their website.

Superannuation ('super')

While I hope that every person who sells their business as their retirement plan makes a squillion dollars and retires happy, there is always a possibility that this won't be the case.

In 2019, just before COVID-19 hit Australia, the survival rate of businesses was between 86% and 89% nationally. In 2023, it was between 62% and 68%. Between AI and tech advancements, how do we know what the future holds? The internet has only been public for just over 30 years and look what that did. Maybe someone else will revolutionise your industry or make it extinct. We simply cannot predict the unpredictable.

If you're a sole trader, a partner in a partnership or a director of a company (not employed), you aren't obliged to pay your own super. Paying your super is hard to commit to, especially when you're first starting out. For many small businesses, there are lots of bills and not a lot of cash. A lot of company owners don't even start drawing a wage for the first 12 to 24 months.

I know it's hard to think about, particularly if you're a small business owner with no other source of income, and I am sorry to keep ramming this home when I'm certain you have other problems to solve. However, your superannuation needs to be a 'now' focus rather than a 'future' focus.

I ran some quick numbers through the Moneysmart superannuation calculator. Consider these figures:

Age 30, starting balance of $5000, with balanced fees and balanced investment.

After-tax contributions:
$100 per month until 67 – $60,594.
$200 per month until 67 – $126,773.
$400 per month until 67 – $259,132.

Age 50, starting balance of $20,000 (four times the amount above), with balanced fees and balanced investment.

After-tax contributions:
$100 per month until 67 – $47,125.
$200 per month until 67 – $72,196.
$400 per month until 67 – $122,338.

See what a difference even small amounts (which could be less than the government's compulsory contribution for regular employees) make? Even if you start with $25 a week and increase it later, time is the secret to your success. We have a whole chapter on super coming up, so if you feel like you don't know much about it, I'm going to explain how it's like cheese fondue, so hang in there.

The simplest budgeting method for your business

This is a simple budgeting tool you can use for your business, especially when you're first starting out. You might find that your accountant or bookkeeper has a different approach, but I love the stacking method of this style.

Your budgeting ladder

While I still think a mind map is excellent for running a business, especially if you don't have a bookkeeper, I also love using the ladder method with small business clients. Not only does a ladder help you focus on one step at a time, but it also has small gaps between the rungs, keeping you motivated. (Of course, you can still use the mind map method. Just add your extra bubbles as rungs and name them according to your personal account vibes. Or, if your personal and business accounts stay separate, you can have two mind maps.)

There are four rungs on the ladder and they are split to cover survival, buffer, goals and spoils. I highly recommend setting up different bank accounts for your different rungs so you're clear on where you're parking your money and why. Let's look at each one in turn.

First rung: the lung rung (survival)

This rung is the lungs of your business. It's what keeps your business alive and breathing. The lung rung amount is your bare minimum costs to keep your business running (as applicable): insurance, rent, utilities, wages, tax, phone/web, suppliers and subscriptions. Ideally, your super is in your lowest rung, too. If you can't afford to put away 12% of your earnings for super, do 5%. If you can't afford 5%, do $20 or $5. In some capacity, at least, our business is for our future self, too, and she deserves a little something, wouldn't you agree?

If you're using your business as your main source of income, you need to factor all your necessary personal expenses into this rung, too. These are all the expenses we discussed in Chapter 15, such as your rent, utilities, food, medical costs, pet care etc.

Whatever time period you calculate your rung for (fortnightly, monthly, quarterly), that's your target. If you aren't hitting that rung, you need to start looking at either reducing the costs in the rung, increasing your earnings to meet the rung, or getting off the ladder.

Some businesses don't have regular fixed sums coming in, so even getting to the first rung can be a struggle. You'll have to fight like hell to stay on the ladder. Of course, there will be times when you don't meet the rung and you have to do some financial moving and shaking to get by. Other times you'll go way over your rung. The next rung can help with this too.

If you're looking at starting a business, it's a huge advantage to have two to three months of estimated lowest-rung expenses ready and set aside, on top of your start-up costs (your buffer rung). This can tide you over during the lean times and while things are getting started. If this isn't possible, that's okay, too, but know your numbers so you can get off the ladder if you need to.

Finally, while it can be scary to sit down and work out your lung rung, it's not as scary as *not* knowing and trying to wing your upcoming costs. Knowing your numbers will empower you in your business and the decisions you make, so don't shy away from them.

Second rung: the unsung hero rung (buffer)

This is the rung that steps up to the microphone when you need someone to save the day. It's an amount you keep aside for when you've had an invoice come in, it's been a big month and you're conscious that it can't last forever, or you've had to dip into your existing buffer and you're trying to replenish it.

I can't advise how much to keep in this rung. It depends on your needs, risk tolerance, and business incomings and outgoings. This rung acts as a buffer and a nice little box tick once your minimums are met. Your goal might be two to three months of estimated lower-rung expenses for those leaner months that all businesses go through when starting out. You can work towards it as a percentage, or as a dollar amount. You don't have to pour everything into your buffer rung, but a healthy one will help ease the mental space your business takes up in your brain.

Let's say you have $300 over and above your lung rung for the month. You could put the whole $300 in your unsung hero rung, or you could just put 50% in and use the rest on the third and fourth rungs, which are up next. Again, it depends on you. If your buffer account is already super flush for your needs and mental comfort, you might skip adding to this rung. You can always bring it back in if you need it down the track.

Third rung: the young rung (choose your own adventure: goal or reward)

The next two rungs keep you young at business heart – inspired, spoiled and excited. The third rung is your threshold for a bit of fun. You can choose your own adventure, whether that's rewarding your hard work or putting money aside for a particular business goal you're working towards. Pick one of those for the third rung and the other one for the fourth rung. You can also be flexible with the amounts, though it will depend on if you're running your business as a side hustle or your main income, as well as how much more you're bringing in above your lung rung and unsung hero rungs.

Your goal might be having a marketing budget, buying the shop next door, hiring a staff member or paying for Canva Pro. Most businesses have some goal to help their growth, and as I always say, your goal doesn't have to look like anyone else's. If you're doing treats first – love it. You've taken care of business – literally – with your lung rung and unsung hero rung. It's therefore more than okay for your third rung to be about spoiling yourself.

Fourth rung: the young rung 2.0 (flip the table)

Whichever one you didn't do for the third rung, add it here. Did you do your goal first? Then it's time to give yourself a little treat. Did you treat yourself first? Then tuck the rest towards your second young rung.

You could also do a 50/50 split with anything above your second buffer rung and do both at the same time. Again, some people like smashing a goal quickly. Some people like to taste the fruits of their labour with rewards. And some people like to do a bit of both.

Note from Bianca at OH Accounting: onwards and upwards

Your ladder can have more than four rungs. This is where some planning for your business can go a long way. Do you want to add other goals or aim for greatness? If your business is stable and surviving, now it's time to thrive. Keep climbing and stepping up.

Mental comfort: risk profiles

People will look at their ladder in different ways. Some are happy to climb; others are afraid of heights. Mental comfort and risk aversion have a lot to do with this, and we don't talk about this enough when we discuss money decisions.

Have you ever noticed that some of your friends or family members are better at taking risks than you? Like, they have a go at things and trust themselves and the process? Sometimes it works out and sometimes it doesn't, but they'll throw themselves into it anyway.

It's not just about money, either, but also sport, travel and business. When it comes to risk tolerance, some people will jump on a plane with no accommodation and a 'no worries' attitude, while others have an 'if we don't have accommodation, we're not going on a trip' attitude, and everything in between. A shout-out to the 'no worries' crowd who are perfectly willing to risk it for the biscuit.

I find these people remarkable because I am the opposite. I am a worrier. A warrior of the worries, if you will. If someone around me is about to take a risk, my voice is saying 'Hell, yes' to them, while my inner voice is going 'Wow, I am scared for this person. What if it doesn't work?' Thankfully, I have mostly trained myself to not say this part out loud.

When it comes to business, your risk aversion is probably going to impact your decision-making, such as when your buffer (unsung hero) rung is full, how much money you have aside before you launch your business and how hard and fast you launch it. There is no right or wrong. It's about what keeps your mental safety in check.

You can (and should) consider others' opinions, but also consider their risk tolerance. If they are at the opposite end of the spectrum, taking their advice without applying your own risk analysis could lead to a meltdown.

Bonus: top tips from an accountant – Bianca Bristow, OH Accounting

Asset protection is a great thing, but to retrospectively address it is much harder, so it's important to chat to the professionals (i.e. your accountant at a minimum and lawyer if it's needed for your industry) at the start if this is something you want to pursue seriously.

Always keep business money separate from personal money. Not only are you going to save in future bookkeeping and accounting fees, but if you're doing bookkeeping yourself, you're making your life simpler as, let's face it, running a business is hard enough.

Cash is king. If you can't afford it with cash, can you really afford it? I know there are always extra things that you have to finance in extreme circumstances, but you need to factor these into your lung rung, otherwise you're setting future you up for a world of pain.

Don't forget the power of terms and conditions (particularly in a service-based business) and make sure they're used right from the start to protect you from any deals going sour – and there will always be one, trust me.

A final note on owning a business

I asked my Instagram followers what their favourite things were about owning a business. This is what they said:

- The freedom to be with my kids when they really need their mummy by their side.
- Autonomy and freedom to say 'no, thanks' to clients I don't want to work with.
- The deepest chats all day every day. No small talk.
- The freedom and flexibility and the ability to be creative and innovative to solve problems.
- There is no limit to what I can earn and there is no glass ceiling.
- Being able to set my own hours.

When I asked about the hardest things, this is what they said:

- Pretty much everything else.
- The constant pressure.
- The lack of boundaries.

- Paying tax (!!!).
- The constant worry about money.
- The battle between personal and business life.
- Cashflow and variable income.
- Having to solve your own problems.
- Lack of flexibility and no holidays.
- Being solely responsible for money.

It's interesting how many of these are some people's positives and other people's negatives. There's no question that running a business is a roller-coaster of sheer excitement and sheer panic. I've had plenty of clients and friends whose businesses didn't work out, and others who've been a roaring success.

A lot of people believe that running a successful business is a fantastic way to build wealth, and they can be right. Others believe that running a business takes up a lot of time and money and that can distract from building wealth, and they're also right.

It's for you to decide. Consider your risk tolerance. Consider dipping your toe in the water before swimming in the ocean. Most people I know who successfully transitioned to their own business prepped beforehand and built over time while still working or being supported by a second income. Finally, realistically consider your costs and don't short-change yourself because you're optimistic. Most importantly, plan your budget and pay your taxes.

Paella

Think long and hard about whether you can afford to *not* get personalised accounting advice.

―――――――――

Consider what business type is best for you. Get advice to

make sure and avoid undoing your hard work later on.

_____

If you're starting a business, invest time in working out your start-up and ongoing costs. Find people with a similar business or structure and ask about their experiences, including unforeseen costs.

_____

Open separate bank accounts – as many as you need to make sure your bills, tax and government obligations are paid, and that you have some cash flow.

_____

Draw or write out your ladder and your rungs, including the order you're using and the amounts you need and/or want in each rung.

 # Reflective questions

If I'm considering starting a business, how does it sit with my risk tolerance?

Have I planned for the costs of my business?

What does my ladder look like for my business?

What are my priorities in my business?

Do I have my support team in place?

Chapter 19

How to crush your bloody debt

There is nothing quite as soul-sucking as unmanageable or barely manageable debt. Somehow, you start with one debt – maybe a credit card, personal loan or overdue bill – and you end up with a few all over the place and direct debits coming out left, right and fucking centre. It feels like every time you try to tread water, some kind of money crisis rears its (always ugly) head and pulls you back under like a rip. On top of that, you feel a crushing sense of shame about your debts and how they seem to get out of control while your back is turned.

I am passionate about crushing any debt that's bothering you because I've seen firsthand the peace that comes over a person when they have the right strategy for them, even before the debts have cleared.

To start on your debt payment journey, you have to be ready to do the other work – your financial coaching, your budget – to prevent you from going back into debt. All the debt paydown methods in the world won't stop you from getting back into debt if you're not doing the supporting work, too.

Getting into debt is a hell of a lot easier than explaining debt. I've tried to give the best context with the least detail. After all, you want to pay off your debt rather than understand how it works. But like knowing your competition in order to defeat them, knowing about debt types will help you to feel more in control about getting rid of them.

Key terms

It's important to understand some key terms before we jump into the types of debt we're dealing with:

- **Principal:** The original amount you owe.
- **Interest:** What the lender charges you for borrowing the money.
- **Fees:** Charges that apply, whether that's for late payments, 'administering' your account, your payment method or anything else a company can come up with.
- **Lender:** A company or person lending you money.
- **Creditor:** A person or company you owe money to. Your lenders are all creditors, but not all your creditors are lenders. For example, your electricity company doesn't lend you money, so they aren't a lender, but if you owe them money for your electricity, they are a creditor.

Types of debt

We often talk about credit cards and personal loans as debts but tend to exclude a lot of other things. After talking about the different types of debts, we'll make a list of yours, so keep that in mind as we go through. Understanding debt types is going to help you identify which ones are most important for paying down your (s)hit list. If you see a financial counsellor or one of the options I discuss later in the chapter, understanding these debt types and which ones you have will be helpful for both of you.

Credit cards

Credit cards are the most common thing we think of when it comes to 'bad debt' – from sneaky sales tactics to statements that offer a tiny minimum payment and an invitation to deal with the consequences at a later date. Credit cards offer you access to a set limit of the bank's money. (You can get credit cards from non-bank lenders, but for ease, I've just used 'bank' as a collective term.) You can either pay the funds back in full during the allocated interest-free days or more slowly with interest.

While credit cards can be used to your advantage, this is the exception, not the rule. If the banks didn't profit from the vast majority of cards, why would they offer them in the first place? It's very easy to get caught up in the 'success stories' of people using credit cards successfully because the people who don't use them successfully don't talk about it very often.

The thing is, people who use credit cards successfully don't need them. They either have enough for what they want or have developed the discipline to wait for it. It's when someone takes a credit card out 'just in case' or to tide them over that it becomes a problem. They haven't been taught the skills to treat credit like the dangerous animal it is.

If you have credit card debt, you aren't alone and there isn't anything wrong with you. It happens more often than you think. Credit cards are set up to make people fail at using them so the bank can keep getting those interest payments.

Personal loans

This is a loan for something personal (a shock, I know). You need to give a reason when applying for a personal loan – such as a holiday, renovations, a car etc. You agree to pay back the amount over a certain time period, with interest and any other fees that apply.

There are two types of personal loans: a secured personal loan and an unsecured personal loan. A secured personal loan is when you get a personal loan for an asset (a 'thing') such as a car or boat. The bank will offer you a lower rate, but they reserve the right to take back the 'thing' if you stop making the payments or fall too far behind. An unsecured loan is when there is no 'thing' for the loan, or the bank cannot take the 'thing' back if you fall too far behind on your payments. This usually applies to holidays or renovations.

Buy now pay later (BNPL)

Think Afterpay, Zip Pay, Klarna and humm. These products offer 'interest-free' plans for balances up to a certain amount, but it has various other fees instead, such as late fees, dishonour fees etc. A number of companies also offer a higher limit with interest, similar to a credit card. It's very easy to get in over your head after being enticed with 'no interest'.

Utility debts

If your water, gas, electricity or phone/internet bills become overdue, these are also debts.

Personal debts

If you owe money to friends, family or housemates, these are also debts.

Vet, car and school debts

Vet bills can sometimes be through a BNPL provider, or can be owed directly to the vet. You can owe debts if you have a car accident (when you're uninsured) and get billed by the other person's insurer. Things like your own insurance and registration normally get cancelled if you don't pay them, rather than becoming a debt. You can still add them to your debt list if you know you can't afford to pay them and they're coming up soon. Overdue school fees also count as debt.

Debt collectors and debt buyers

Sometimes, a creditor will outsource your debt to someone else. Either they pay a company to 'collect' the debt on their behalf for a fee or commission (debt collector), or they sell the debt to another company, very cheaply, and give them the chance to get the money out of the person instead (debt buyer). You can owe money to a debt collector or a debt buyer for one of your other debts.

Government debts

ATO debts, Child Support debts or Centrelink overpayment debts are usually the main ones here.

Housing debts

If you rent and you're behind in your payments, your debt is called being 'in arrears' or 'past due' and you should include what is overdue as a debt.

Your mortgage is a debt, but generally we would only include it on your debt paydown list if you're behind in your repayments, which is also called being in arrears.

For now, if you're up-to-date on your housing and have other debts, leave housing off the list. If you have mortgage or rent arrears (outstanding payments), these will need to go at the top of your 'category one' list, which we'll be talking about in a minute.

Higher Education Contribution Scheme (HECS) debt

HECS-HELP and FEE-HELP are government study loans. The balance goes up every year with inflation (this is called indexing), but you aren't charged interest. The repayments you have to make, which start once you earn enough to reach a certain threshold, will come out of your pay automatically as long as you let payroll know you have a HECS debt.

If you want to add study debt to your debt paydown list, you can, but considering you don't get harassed to pay more than the bare minimum and don't get charged fees, you'll probably have it quite low on the list. Or, you can exclude it and let it tick down in the background. Your HECS will be a low-priority debt if you have others to take care of.

Your debt (s)hit list

Now it's time to build your list – the (s)hit list of debts you are going to pay down, and in what order. I've had every type of list come into my office, from handwritten notes and colour-coded spreadsheets to screenshots from a notes app. It doesn't matter how you do it, just *do* it. Here's how to order them:

Category One

1. Housing debt (rent or mortgage arrears)
2. Other secured loans, including car loans
3. Utility debts
4. Any other debts for which you have been issued a 'default' notice.

Your 'Category One' list should look like the following:

Creditor	Type	Arrears/ Overdue	Total Amount	Notes (including minimum payments)
Hanky Bank	Home loan	$38,588	$568,000	*Soon to issue default notice*
Baa Baa Cars	Car loan	$1,200	$23,000	*Not sure on status*
Carved Energy	Gas bill	$300	$300	*Disconnection notice received*

Category Two

The order of your Category Two items is less important – you'll see why when we get to the strategies. This list will include all your unsecured debts that you want to pay down. The list is only slightly different.

Creditor	Type	Arrears/ Overdue	Interest Rate/Fees	Notes (including minimum payments)
Slap Credit	Credit card	$18,000	21%	*minimum payment $212 a month*
Baa Baa Cars	Buy Now Pay Later x 3	$1,200	$8 + $38 + $20 late fees	*Three purchases – hate this company!!!*
Mum	Private Loan	$300	$0%	*Happy to wait until last*

Overview of options

Now we're going to talk about how to deal with your debts, depending on where you're at.

Category One

Category One is very tricky. For example, it depends on how long you have been in arrears for. If you have been issued with a 'default notice' for your mortgage or car loan, a 'termination due to breach' for your rent, or a 'disconnection notice' from your utility providers, get in touch with a financial counsellor urgently. A financial counsellor looks at all your options holistically, meaning they will look outside your debts and consider any government entitlements or hardship programs that you may be eligible for. Plus, they're free, confidential and independent. I've got information on what financial counsellors help with and how to access one later in this section. The same advice applies if you have other loans secured against your house, including loans or 'personal guarantees'. Financial counsellor, asap.

Because Category One is very dependent on your personal circumstances, I can't give you a strategy for how to tackle it. If you have a Category One list, you should be talking with a financial counsellor to see what options suit your specific situation, even if you have some plans in place. Writing your Category One list in advance will help, or a financial counsellor can help you write one.

Category Two

Here's a flow chart of the options we're going to work through for Category Two debts:

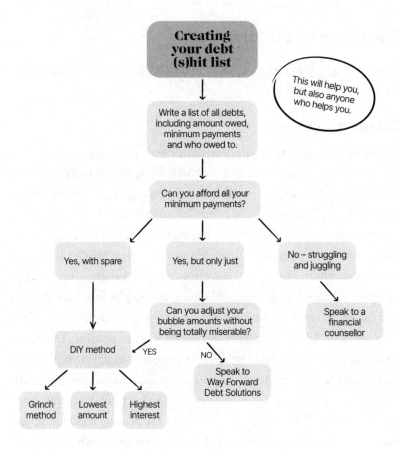

If you can't make your minimum payments, especially if you have low income or you're struggling to get your bills paid, a financial counsellor is for you. As I said before, they look at all options holistically, meaning they will look outside your debts as well. Plus, they're free, confidential and independent.

If you have an okay income and you know you can pay something towards your debts, just not the full amount (or only by the skin of your teeth), and you haven't been able to save, it's worth having a chat with Way Forward Debt Solutions. Way Forward is a charity that supports people who have overcommitted but have some capacity to pay. The Way Forward team does some incredible work.

If you're meeting your minimums with money to spare, we'll talk about the DIY methods you can work through later in the chapter.

As always, rather than giving you the one-and-only way, you've got plenty of choices so you can use the method that's best for you. Let's talk about each of these a bit more.

Here's what a financial counsellor can help with:

- issues managing debt
- repayment plans
- Centrelink entitlements
- negotiating with creditors
- budgeting
- utility hardship programs
- bankruptcy
- referrals.

Here's what a financial counsellor generally can't help with:

- legal advice
- tenancy assistance
- providing finance, credit or loans (except government-funded loan programs)
- for-profit companies that make budgets for you
- debt consolidation loans.

How do I access a financial counsellor?

Financial counsellors generally work in non-profit agencies throughout Australia. Before you find one, it's worth speaking to the National Debt Helpline. Firstly, a representative will have a preliminary conversation with you to make sure financial counselling is the service you need. It's hard enough having conversations about your personal circumstances without going to the wrong type of service. Also, it's sometimes easier to have a first conversation when you aren't looking at someone directly. The National Debt Helpline also has an online chat service that can be great if you hate making calls. The number is 1800 007 007 and the website is ndh.org.au.

Way Forward Debt Solutions

I've witnessed Way Forward change my clients' lives and I'll sing their praises with every breath. It's similar to a debt management firm (DMF), except it's free. It's also a charity rather than a for-profit business. Banks and other creditors donate to Way Forward to be able to partner with them. The banks benefit because customers who may not have made any payments can start paying *something*. It also means Way Forward can negotiate on your behalf to reduce your balance and repayments with creditors. You then make one payment to Way Forward and they make the repayments to your creditors on your behalf. The payment plans are normally structured across five to seven years.

Way Forward usually works with unsecured debts, but it'll do what it can to help with everything else. If Way Forward assesses that you won't be able to work under its payment plans, it'll refer you to a financial counsellor for further help. Way Forward provides a free, client-centred alternative to DMFs. It has my heart for the great work it does.

Be wary of 'for-profit' debt help companies. There are companies that offer themselves as specialists to help sort your debts for a fee. This might be through consolidation loans, binding agreements or them negotiating payment plans on your behalf. These companies often charge like a wounded bull for these services. They generally get an upfront fee (I've had clients who paid $5000) and/or take a cut of the repayments made to the creditors.

What I'll say is this: I've had a number of clients over the years who signed up with these services, paid their fees and still ended up in my financial counselling office when it went wrong. If you are considering signing up with a fee-for-service company to manage your debts, please speak to a financial counsellor and/or Way Forward first – both of which are free.

DIY methods

If you're able to make your minimum payments on everything and have some extra money to start knocking these debts out of Ivy Park, you can work through your (s)hit list as you like. I've outlined three different options below:

- The Grinch method.
- The lowest amount first – this will help you progress fastest.
- The highest interest first – this will save you the most money.

My favourite is the Grinch method, so we'll start there.

Grinch method

Rather than a prescriptive method, like choosing the debt with the lowest amount or highest interest, I always ask clients, 'Which debt bothers you the most?' or 'Which one do you hate, hate, hate, loathe entirely?' Maybe it's the oldest one, or they inherited it from their ex, or the company just hounds them non-stop to pay what's owed. If they've got a debt like that, I always suggest working on that one first, because that's going to be the most satisfying. Yes, paying off the one with the highest interest first might save you some cash, but nothing beats the feeling of getting rid of the one that makes you clench your jaw every time you think about it. As much as logic plays a part in our money, our emotions play a bigger role.

Case study: Yasmin, 37

Yasmin came to financial counselling with six different unsecured debts of varying amounts, from $300 to $42,000. As we were talking about potential ways to look at getting them paid off – Yasmin was a high-income earner and had the capacity to make payments – we went through what it would look like if we focused on smallest to largest, or if we did lowest interest to highest interest. Yasmin was resigned but not excited. When I asked her what we were missing, Yasmin said one of the debts in the middle of both lists was one that she hated thinking about. She hated the way the company hounded her when she was in financial difficulty and personal crisis, and she was exhausted thinking about how long it would take to get that one paid off. So, we put that one at the top of the list and Yasmin focused all her energy on getting it gone, including selling some of her old shoes and bags to put lump sums down. This was the catalyst; once this was done the biggest weight was off her shoulders and she became determined to tackle the rest.

Lowest amount first

Reorder your list from the smallest to the largest. Focus on getting that first sucker paid off. Once the first one is gone, take the payment amount you were making on the first one and apply that to the second one – in addition to the payment you were already making. Continue to the third one, and so on.

Highest interest first

Often favoured by STEM folks and other logical babes, this is similar to the method above, but instead of the lowest amount, you order them from the highest interest to the lowest interest. This is the most financially efficient, and if that's what makes your brain feel good, go for it. Again, it doesn't matter how you do it, just do it.

Negotiating your debts

It's always worth calling your creditors to see if they can help you get your debts either up-to-date or paid off faster. Here are some negotiation tips:

- Ask open-ended questions, like 'How can you help me with this?' If you get a negative response, respond with 'What other options can you give me?'
- Always be polite. People are not the company they work for.
- Every bank or creditor has their own assessment criteria and process. You might get a great result from one and no result from another.
- You're less likely to get a result from a secured debt – but it's still worth a try.
- If you're willing to close your BNPL or credit card, these

creditors will often consider stopping any further interest or fees to allow you to make a long-term payment arrangement for the remaining balance.

- If you're in financial difficulty, the more honest you are about your situation, the more likely you are to get the right kind of assistance. Financial difficulty teams, for the most part, have come a long way, and are specially trained to have an 'empathy first' approach when they work with you.

- Creditors might want to see your income and expenses, as well as your other debts. This is called a 'statement of financial position'. You've already done the hard part with your debt list. The Australian Financial Complaints Authority (AFCA) has an excellent digital template that every creditor should be familiar with. Otherwise, the bank will send you their template. Tip: the first time you fill one out, make sure you keep a copy of the information in case you need to fill out a different one, or a creditor asks you questions about things that are on it.

- If you receive a lump sum from anywhere (inheritance, tax return, separation, remediation) and have multiple debts, make an appointment with a financial counsellor to have a chat about reduced offers of settlement. This is where you offer each creditor a lower amount than the full balance but in proportion to the lump sum.

- If you believe the creditor has done the wrong thing by you, make a complaint and ask for a review. If you still aren't satisfied, ask the creditor if they're a member of any external dispute resolution scheme – such as AFCA or an ombudsman, and make a complaint there.

It's not about how you do it but that you *are* doing it. The hardest part about paying off your debts is making a start, but once you find the solution – whether it's DIY or with support – you'll never look back.

Hotcakes with syrup

(takeaways) from Chapter 19

Write your full debt list into a table, including everything.

_____

Follow the (s)hit list flow chart and assess your next course of action.

_____

If needed, speak to a financial counsellor or Way Forward, but avoid fee-for-service companies.

_____

If you're doing it yourself, choose the best paydown method for you, and order your list accordingly.

_____

Keep paying your minimums and focus your energy on the debt at the top of your list until it's gone.

Reflective questions

How am I going to reward myself for sitting down and getting my debt list written out?

Are there any debts I should focus on first, such as rent/ mortgage arrears, utilities or a secured car loan?

Do I need to speak to a financial counsellor or Way Forward? Or am I going to DIY it?

Which debt paydown method resonates with me?

What is my Grinch debt?

If I was going to pick a debt to negotiate, which one would it be?

Chapter 20

You can't reheat your leftovers if the container is empty

There are two ways to create more room in your budget: spend less or earn more. While that sounds straightforward, it doesn't consider the multitude of factors that may make one or the other impossible for you.

It borders on arrogance to tell a nurse who is working 60 hours a week and coming home to kids who need taking care of that they simply need to earn more and spend less. Or to tell someone with a chronic illness or disability to increase their hours or get a first or second job.

Only you know what you have the capacity to consider, and that might change over time. Maybe you'll have more capacity, maybe you'll have less. It also depends on your needs. Do you need substantial extra income on a consistent basis to make ends meet? Or can you do bits and bobs for pleasure to support one of your goals or one of your debts?

Earning more

If you know you have some capacity to look at ways to earn more, I've provided some ideas – from clients, people I know and personal experience. They do have some overlap, and these lists are not exhaustive. Your limit is your creativity – and your research. Just remember, if you're earning extra income, you need to pay tax on that income. If you aren't sure, speak to an accountant.

Gig economy

From Airtasker to events work, the gig economy refers to work that is mostly done by subcontractors and casuals rather than full-time staff. It's flexible and you can work within your skill set or try something new. You don't generally get sick leave or annual leave. If you do the work as a casual staff member, you don't have an Australian Business Number (ABN) and your employer should take out tax. As a contractor, you'll usually have an ABN.

Examples

Fiverr, Airtasker, rideshare and food delivery all operate in the gig economy, but there are other ways, too. I used to work as an usher at a couple of stadiums in Perth as a second casual job. An old colleague of mine had a band that used to play at weddings and events – also part of the gig economy.

Business

If you're a subcontractor in the gig economy, you'll have an ABN and therefore your own business. However, you can also have a business where you provide goods and/or services to people or other businesses. You'll need to consider set-up costs, what gap in the market you are aiming to fill, and if you're actually in with a shot at making a profit and after how long. A lot of people aren't able to pay themselves a wage in the beginning, so if you need extra income in the short-term, consider whether your business will provide that.

Examples

I've done copywriting work through my business, and I also use it for my student mentoring and book-related income and expenses. Deline from Mazi Wealth has her own financial planning business. My friend Megan from Self Care Studio Maylands has her own gender-inclusive beauty salon. From delivering courses to making candles, the world is your oyster. Just make sure you run your numbers to understand whether this is a helpful option at this stage of your journey.

Leveraging your current job

Depending on what you do, there are often ways you can leverage your job or job skills to earn more money – whether that's working overtime or doing work that is aligned with your qualifications or other skills. It could even be keeping detailed track of your outcomes and performance throughout the year to justify a position change or pay rise, or hunting down another job. In one of my previous jobs, we didn't have annual performance reviews, so I made my own and called a meeting every year with my boss to discuss my achievements and my value to the business. Brazen, I know, but there was no harm in asking and it worked every time.

Examples

I have a friend who works as a government vet. She does casual private vet shifts on the weekend, and extra pet-sitting. An old colleague found the same job she was doing at a different agency and moved for a substantial pay rise. I've done some casual teaching for the university where I'm studying for my law degree and I'm also mentoring/tutoring a private student. I also sell my first-year notes online.

Miscellaneous

Whether it's selling your stuff on Depop/eBay/Gumtree/Facebook Marketplace, or contributing to container deposit schemes, there are so many ways to make extra money every now and again without the pressure of being rostered or having deadlines.

Examples

Canna Campbell from SugarMamma does all sorts of things, from surveys and market research to selling/buying second-hand luxury pieces. My friend Stacie buys and sells killer designer clothes she finds at op shops. The other day I saw someone selling lemons at the front of their house – three for $1. I've done house-sitting and cat-sitting. Maybe I'll branch out to dog-walking – who knows.

You may have automatically dismissed some of these ideas, but if you have the capacity, I recommend you try your hand at a few things, even if it's just to stimulate your brain to work in a different way. Tell yourself that you are 'open to opportunities' to make more money and see what shakes out. It might be totally different to what you were expecting.

If you are on a Centrelink payment, make sure you check how much you can earn without experiencing any impacts to your payments – especially for Childcare Subsidy and/or Family Tax Benefit.

Spending less

Groceries

Grocery shopping is my biggest can't-be-bothered area. I try to keep my weekly shop under a certain amount, but I refuse to go to three shops every week for my groceries. When I'm buying for myself, it's very much a case of efficiency. However, I worked with a financial counsellor who is the queen of saving money on her grocery shop – Deb Laidler. I asked her for her top tips:

- Never shop hungry.
- Plan meals using what is in your fridge and pantry first.
- Check unit prices to make sure you aren't paying more for less.
- Plan meals for your leftovers. Roast chicken one night and then leftovers in soup or pasta bake the next.
- Cook once, eat twice. Make mince mix for spaghetti and then nachos or tacos – or freeze the second serve for when you need a quick fix.
- Store your food properly so it lasts.
- Grate your own cheese.
- Buy bulk if you have the money and the freezer space.

Housing

Housing is one of the hardest categories. Between the rental crisis and the cost of buying property, there are very limited options for spending less in housing. However, there are things you can think about. If you don't have kids, can you get a housemate? Or would you consider sucking it up and share housing – especially if you're saving for something important? It can also be looking within the home. Audit your subscriptions for streaming and all the tag-alongs (VPN, grocery delivery etc.). Consider your utilities. An electric blanket and a pair of Uggs can mean not having the heater on day and night. Get things like your fridge seals and garden sprinklers checked. You likely spend a lot of time at home, and it's about what you're willing to sacrifice and what you aren't. There's no right and wrong that applies to everyone.

Bills

As we discussed in Chapters 12 and 14, setting up BPAY or direct debit payments in smaller amounts weekly or fortnightly instead of monthly or quarterly makes budgeting easier. Plus, with things like your mortgage and credit card, you'll end up saving interest because you make an extra payment in the year (26 fortnightly payments versus 12 monthly ones).

Bills such as utilities and insurance need at least an annual check-up. I do mine in January and February as this is when I receive my renewals but also when I do life admin, such as going to the dentist. Ideally, your irregular expenses account will allow you to build up enough over time to pay your insurances annually as you normally get a decent discount on car/home/pet insurance when paying in full.

While you can always go for the cheapest option, some things are worth staying loyal to. My car insurance company gives flawless service and it would have to be a *big* price difference for me to consider leaving. You might get phenomenal service from your small internet provider, and to me, that's worth paying extra for.

Think about what works for you

Your best cost-saving strategies will develop as you become better acquainted with your values. For example, I hate clutter (except for books). I haven't owned a printer in years. To me, they're expensive and ugly space-fillers. When I print my assignments or anything else, I go to Officeworks. I'll use the fuel apps to find the best deal on petrol. But I don't save as much as I could on grocery shopping because the energy it would take is not a strategic or exciting use of my time. Some people will DIY house maintenance and repairs. Some couples will drop to one car. Some people delay starting their washing machine until 3am to save peak costs on electricity or do it during the day using solar power. Some people sign up for cashback websites and membership programs. Again, being 'open to opportunities' will surprise you.

How to tell your friends you don't have the budget

Times are pretty tough right now, and a lot of people who had a savings cushion are using it. Despite all this, conversations about money when you're the person who has less to spend are really hard. Whether it comes from trauma, embarrassment or resentment, this part is about practical strategies you can implement right now, rather than doing a deep dive into healing yourself.

Personal money dynamics are different for everyone, whether it's between friends, family members or colleagues. A good approach is called the 'lie, why or sigh' methodology. It's a three-level system that gives you tools to use at whatever stage you're at.

The lie method

It's common for people to say, 'If you can't tell your friends you can't afford it, why are they your friends?' This is unhelpful. Relationships with ourselves and others are complex, so it's okay if you need to lie because you're not quite ready to have those hard conversations. This is what it might look like:

- 'I'm exhausted from work at the moment and I need a "pizza in pyjamas" night.'
- 'I found a recipe I want to try. Let's do that instead.'
- 'I can't make dinner but I'll come meet you for dessert or a drink.'

The last one is great if your friends split bills evenly and you would normally only get an entrée and a lime soda (thank you for this one, Troy).

The why method

This is technically called the 'find a why'. It helps you develop a reason for yourself, rather than feeling bad about lying. Call it 'truth lite' if you like. It's based on future you and is focused on choosing something you know is coming up that you want to prioritise as important in your conversations. This is what it might look like:

- 'I'm saving for a trip/moving house/buying a new dishwasher/getting my car serviced.'
- 'I've got Emily's/Mum's/Jeff's birthday coming up and I want to do something special.'

The sigh method

The sigh method is where you bite the bullet and just say things as they are (or close to it). This is what it might sound like:

- 'Team, I've got heaps of big expenses coming up. Can we do homemade tacos instead?'
- 'There's a lot in my calendar I need to budget for. Can we just do a grazing board and hang out?'
- 'I can't afford that right now.'

When you're the friend with more to spend

Babes, if you're the wealthy friend, or even just the 'okay right now' friend, check in on your besties. It can really help a struggling friend when someone takes the mental load off by asking the question first. This doesn't have to be a serious heart-to-heart during every catch-up. It can sound like this:

- 'Are we feeling boujee or budget for this catch-up?'
- 'How are our budgets this week? Do we want to just hang out at home?'

Times are tight right now, and whatever method you use, it takes grit to have these conversations. The best tip for all the strategies is to offer an alternative after stating your reason. Rather than leaving awkwardness or room for questions in the group chat, give everyone an alternative they can agree to instead of another thing to think about. By doing this, you've got a much better shot at everything going smoothly.

Fettuccine carbonara

(takeaways) from Chapter 20

Reflect on the 'earn more' ideas and consider how much time and mental space you can commit.

Consider what plays to your strengths, and be wary of extra income traps that cost more than they bring in.

Look through the 'spend less' examples and see if anything jumps out at you, or use them as a guide to inspire different ideas.

Try one thing first, then add another, rather than making sweeping changes and trying multiple strategies together.

Reflective questions

Do I have the time and mental capacity to earn more?
What would that look like for me? Do I need to get any advice about it?

Do I have the time and mental capacity to spend less?
What would that look like for me? Do I need to get any advice about it?

What method can I use to tell my friends I don't have the budget?

Do I need to be more mindful about checking on my friends' budgets?

Chapter 21

Superannuation – rich, mysterious aunty energy

We either know her or dream about being her. She's the rich, vivacious aunty who has a suspicious amount of money, remains silent in the family group chat (because she simply doesn't care about the day-to-day drama) and gives you amazing birthday gifts before telling you about the fantastic holiday she just went on. Babes, welcome to your superannuation.

Your superannuation is like this aunty because if you do her right, she'll lurk in the background for years and deliver the goods when it comes to retirement. For most of us, traditional retirement is bloody far away (is it, though?), but retired you wants the good life too and she's asking you to get your shit together.

'Hang the fuck on,' you may say. 'I thought superannuation was that crusty finance thing that stockbrokers, retirees and politicians bang on about?' That's what the super industry wants you to think. Because if you don't understand it, it's easier for them to make plenty of money off you.

The basics of superannuation shouldn't be as hard to understand as they are. But as soon as you start talking about the basics, there's context that needs to wrap around it. It is, as my cousin Cameron describes it, 'user hostile'. Like an onion, super has lots of flavour, but it's ready to bring you to tears at any moment. Luckily, by the time you finish this chapter, you'll be 'that bitch' when it comes to superannuation.

The 12-step Aunty Sue program

You can do this as a 12-week program, a 12-month program or a 12-hour program if you like. There are only some steps that require 'action' from you – they're marked with an asterisk. Each step builds on the other until you're a glorious Aunty Sue all off your own back. Even if you only do some of these steps, you'll still be making progress, and when it comes to superannuation, progress literally makes you money. The more interested you are, the more money you can make without spending anything. Are you starting to get a sense of why I love Aunty Sue so bloody much?

Understanding your super, even if it takes time, empowers you now and in the future. Plus, you can't escape it, so you may as well get across it.

Step 1. What is super and how does it work?

Once we retire, we aren't earning wages anymore and we need something to live off. Enter rich Aunty Sue(perannuation).

Superannuation is money that gets put aside for retirement. It was set up in 1992 (my vintage – what a year) as a compulsory requirement for people who are working. It's paid by employers from your wages. The compulsory percentage has changed over the years, but it's due to reach 12% by July 2025. You can also add money into your super if you choose. Super funds manage lots of people's money to make sure it doesn't waste away before they retire.

How does superannuation work?

Your superannuation isn't like a locked-down bank account. The money doesn't get left to earn 3% to 4 % interest (unless it's a 'cash' investment option – more on this shortly). If it did, it would get eaten up over the years because the price of being alive goes up over time, and by more than the usual interest you would earn in a bank account. This is called inflation. Put simply, your money won't go as far in the future as it does today. Consider the effects of inflation over the 20 to 50 years between now and retirement. Yikes.

Your superannuation sits with a pile of other super accounts in the super fund, which is managed by 'fund managers'. Basically, they take everyone's money and invest it in things to make it grow more than that 3% to 4% it would in a bank account. They can put it in all sorts of things – shares, property, bonds, cash or combinations of those. They can invest in Australia and overseas. We'll get into what all that means in a second.

Step 2. Why super is important

Super is important because it forces us to put some money away during our working lives for when we're not working anymore. It also gets invested into things on your behalf to make that money grow so you aren't left with the equivalent of $150 when you retire. It's common to delay thinking about how we'll support ourselves in retirement, which is why it's a real struggle when we finally do look at it. Superannuation helps us prepare early without having to think about it too much.

Step 3. Is your super getting paid?*

If you're working, you need to check that your superannuation is getting paid, not just on your payslip but also in your super account. Set up a member online account for your super fund (ask payroll if you're not sure which fund it is) so that you can log in and check. At the moment, payments have to be made at least quarterly, with proposed legislation to change the requirement so that super has to be paid on the day you get your wages. As it's the law, you'd think that businesses always pay it, but you'd be surprised.

You can make extra voluntary contributions to your super, which can make a huge difference to your balance at retirement. You can do these before tax through salary sacrificing, which means your employer takes it out before you get your wages. These are also called 'concessional contributions' and are taxed at a flat rate of 15%. You can also do them after tax by paying them manually. These are called 'non-concessional contributions'. In some circumstances, you can get a tax deduction for these (because you've already paid tax on the money), but you'll need to contact the ATO to make sure you're eligible and get the forms you need to complete from your super fund.

Remember, any extra money you contribute to your super can't be pulled out again in most circumstances, so be careful about accidentally leaving your budget or savings short in the process. You can test some numbers on the Moneysmart website, or speak to your super fund (or advisor) about voluntary contributions.

Rich Aunty Sue action
Find out who your super is with, create an online account on their website or download the app, and check to make sure money has been paid into your super in the last three months. If not, it's time to email payroll with a 'please explain', and you can report them to the ATO if they still don't pay it.

Step 4. How many super funds do you have?*

It's also worth checking how many super funds you have and how much is in them as a starting point. You can look this up in your myGov account or call the ATO for assistance. Search 'ATO lost super' for more. Having multiple super accounts can work for some people, such as where there are insurance policies in multiple accounts. We want to make sure it's a deliberate choice, because multiple accounts mean you're paying more fees, and over 30 years, they can really add up. We'll talk more about this in Step 9.

Rich Aunty Sue action
Check how many super accounts you have and make a list of them. No other action is required at this time.

Step 5. Understanding key super terms

You know how menus can have all these weird words listed in the dishes and you have to sit there googling what turns out to be a type of lettuce and a herbed crouton? Superannuation has similar nonsense where fancy words are really just lettuce and croutons. We're going to cover some of the weird words on our super menu to save us some time.

Estate

When you die, the things you own – that are worth money – form your 'estate'. I could bore you with the history of the term but it's not that important. Your estate includes any property, shares, savings accounts, vehicles (cars, motorbikes, caravans) and anything like jewellery and designer bags.

Inflation

It's how we measure the costs of things going up over time.

Portfolio

When I was young, I assumed this was an actual portfolio with clear plastic sleeves, like the one you had in year 10 with all your assignments. Bless. Your portfolio is all the things you own that make you money. You can have a portfolio within your super as well as outside of it (don't worry about the outside part for now). It might have things like cash, shares, bonds and property. See 'investment option' below.

Superannuation

Money put aside by your employers and/or you over your working life to pay for expenses when you reach your 'preservation age'.

Preservation age

The age you can access your super. This changes depending on when you were born. At the time of writing, if you're retired and born after 1964, it's 60. It's a bit more complicated than that, but I'll add all the extra stuff at the end so you don't lose your mind if this is the first time you're looking into it.

It's called preservation age because it's 'preserved' until you reach the right age, like beef jerky. There are some circumstances when you can access your superannuation early, but not many. I'll cover those at the end too.

Pension

If you were born after 1957 and reach age 67 – and don't have enough in assets (stuff worth money) and superannuation to retire – you can apply for the Age Pension from the government. It's hardly enough to get by, but it does act as a safety net, especially for people who haven't been able to work a lot or who have earned very little.

Investment option

Like a pick-and-mix candy store, we can choose how our super money gets invested. Some people want only chocolate-based stuff. Some want sour and sweet lollies. Some only want red liquorice. We've got a whole part on this coming up, so get your lolly bag ready.

Risk

Risk is like the gin and tonic of superannuation. The more gin you have, the more fun you might have. However, there is a higher risk of getting hungover, throwing up, having a fuzzy head and/ or saying some things you don't mean. But if you space that gin out over a long period of time, you lessen the risk of those things happening. It's a fine line between feeling relaxed and feeling sick.

Risk in your super (or investing generally, but let's not over-complicate it) is the chance of you losing money because of the things you've invested in. Risk is important to understand because it's not a bad thing so much as it's a thing that you need to be aware of. If you're 20, you can often afford to have more 'risk' in your super as you have far more time for those gin and tonics to pace themselves out. If you're 60 and due to retire in five years, you have much less time. The thing is, the more risk you have, the higher the chance of your superannuation growing.

Frankly, as a very 'risk aware' investor myself, I think they really could have chosen a less scary word, such as 'gin'.

Risk allows our portfolios to grow faster. Remember when we talked about how super works? The growing part allows you to beat inflation at its own sneaky game. If your money is invested conservatively (lots of tonic, minimal gin), it's hard for it to grow.

You don't need to be scared of risk. You just need to under-stand what it means. If you're younger, you have more time for the waves of highs and lows to do their thing. As you get older, it's more likely you need to create fewer waves, especially if you're close to retirement and need that money soon.

MySuper

In 2012, the federal government brought in some laws to force super funds to have a simple default option for new members. MySuper options are generally set up with lower fees and a more basic structure. They're like a pre-packaged cracker/cheese/dip combo from the supermarket that suits most people. If you haven't manually set up your super, it's likely that you're in a MySuper fund. A salute to the government for looking out for those of us in our not-quite-rich-Aunty-Sue era who haven't looked at our super in detail (or at all).

Step 6. Understanding fees

First, let me tell you about the conspiracy theory of superannuation. From 2018 to 2023, there were over 15,000 employees in the super-annuation industry, and the industry's revenue was over $200 billion. While some super funds reinvest their profits back into the fund, most are getting a cut – every year. Of course, people need to get paid, but there are lots of fees being charged in the hope that people won't notice or do anything about them. It's time to be *aggressive* in protecting *your* money from what is sometimes highway robbery (especially when super funds have performed badly). If saving money for retirement doesn't inspire you when you've got bills to pay now, maybe you can be inspired to *fight the system*.

Back to fees. Let me tell you, the fees work hard. Those babies are working overtime, doing the graveyard shift, earning commission – you name it. I'm positive someone at every super fund gets paid $200,000 a year to find new fees and ways to increase the old ones. Let's go over these fees really quickly.

Admin fee

Your basic fee to cover the costs of having people to speak to, running the online platform, sending out statements and stuff like that. This can be a flat fee or a percentage, depending on your fund. Generally, if you have a high balance, a percentage-based administration fee is probably going to cost you more.

Investment fee

This is a fee for managing how your money is invested. It can include lots of different things – brokerage and fees for buying investments, government fees, paying for fund managers etc. Usually a percentage, this fee changes depending on how intense your investment option is. (When I say intense, it means how much effort is involved in managing your investment and why.)

Since the new legislation in 2019, if you have less than $6000 in your super, the fund can only charge you a maximum of 3% for investment fees, admin fees and indirect fees. This figure is still highway robbery, but there we are.

Performance fee

Each investment type will often have a goal or target, sometimes called a key performance indicator (KPI). If a fund meets its target, it can charge you for doing a good job. This is usually a percentage.

Switching fee

Some funds will charge you if you change how your super is invested. It can still be worth it depending on the other fees you pay. Some super funds don't charge. Some charge if you do it more than once a year (or won't let you). Some probably charge you if you say 'switching fee' into a mirror three times in a row, but I haven't tried it, just in case.

Financial advice fee

If you get help on how your superannuation is invested or other advice from one of your fund's financial advisors, they will often charge for this service. This is an additional service and often well worth the cost for the money you'd save because of their advice.

Other fees

Honestly, the horrors persist, depending on your super fund. There can be establishment fees, financial advice fees, 'contribution splitting fees', family law splitting fees and withdrawal fees.

Most of these you can look up on a case-by-case basis on government websites such as Moneysmart and APRA (Australian Prudential Regulation Authority – a fancy way of saying that they make sure banking, insurance and superannuation in Australia are all keeping their noses clean and not doing people dirty).

Super funds often tuck your fees away into your half-yearly statement, a product disclosure statement (PDS) or investment guide that's bloody hard to find (one time it took me 15 minutes to find one I was looking for). They also split all the fees up in different columns so the numbers look small.

A 'high' fee would normally be when your combined investment and performance fees equal more than 1%. You may say, 'You've written a whole chapter about one bloody per cent?' Let me show you why 1% matters.

Consider a 30-year-old who earns $50,000 a year, has a super balance of $35,000 and wants to retire at age 67.

0.5% fees = $97,194 at retirement ($10,298 fees).

1% fees = $91,078 ($16,414 fees).

2% fees = $80,474 ($27,018 fees).

And that's with a $35,000 balance. If her balance was $100,000 and she earned $100k, this would be the difference:

0.5% fees – $203,526 at retirement ($18,251 fees).

1% fees – $190,250 ($31,527 fees).

2% fees – $167,354 ($54,423 fees).

As you can see, 1.5% more means a $36,000 difference in fees. It's a no from me. But before you go bananas on your fund by googling a low-fee super fund and moving all your money to it, stay tuned for the next step.

Rich Aunty Sue action
Wait for the next step.

Step 7. Investment types and investment options*

How your super is invested can have a huge impact on the fees you pay. Earlier, we talked about the different ways your fund manager can invest your super. But what we didn't talk about is that you can have a say in how they do it. This is called your 'investment option'. I'm sorry, I know it's a lot to handle. The fees for the different investment options differ, and by a lot for a couple of different reasons:

- The effort needed by the fund managers who are making decisions about how to invest the money. More effort = more fees.
- The risk of the investment.
- What makes up the portfolio and what it costs to buy and manage those things.

Last time I checked, my super fund had about 18 options. You can call your super fund and make an appointment to speak to one of their financial advisors to work out which one is best for you, or get in touch with a certified financial planner (CFP) or financial advisor who can look at your whole financial position.

I don't like to assume people understand investing, what investments are and how they work. Again, the finance bros have made investing sound like the astrophysics of money, and it gets tired. This book isn't about investing, but we need to cover the basics. Also, it's such a power move to know what finance bros are talking about and being able to see through their shenanigans.

I can't tell you what to do with your super, but I can give you a high-level overview of what things mean so when you start looking at your super you don't get the heebie-jeebies about all the words on the website. We will *not* be outsmarted by jargon.

What are investments?

I've tried to make these as simple as possible. These are the main 'classes' of investments:

- **Cash:** Usually bank deposits that earn some interest. Basically, good old money.
- **Fixed interest:** Usually a stable, fixed-term investment where interest gets paid out after an agreed time. Includes term deposits and bonds. Bonds are normally offered by governments or companies when they want to raise money. They're like a fixed loan that pays you interest.
- **Shares:** Companies that offer shares allow you to buy tiny pieces of the company itself, which they sell to raise money for expansion or other strategic reasons. The shares get bought and sold on the share market (called the ASX in Australia). A company's share price goes up and down depending on its performance, public opinion and local and world events. The whole share market goes up and down, too.

- **Speculative investments:** Includes things such as cryptocurrency and precious metals. You can also get 'speculative shares' within the share market. It's very rare for a super fund to invest in these.

A note on investment types

When we talk about these in the 'investment option' context we're going to talk about next, sometimes the super fund has a mix that doesn't meet the stricter definitions above. For example, a superannuation fund might have a cash option that includes some fixed interest, even though it's called 'cash'.

Investment options: pre-mix versus your own pour

When it comes to the investment options in your super, super funds offer heaps of options from the combinations above. Think of them like charcuterie boards. Some have more cheese; some have more dip; some have celery and carrot sticks.

They normally fall into two categories: pre-mixed and self-selected. It's a bit like getting that gin and tonic from earlier in a can or pouring your own drink. The pre-mixed investment options mean the gin (risk) to soda (conservative) balance is calculated for you. They also have a 'choose your own adventure' investment options section, where you get to choose the amount of gin (risk) and soda (conservative) that you want.

If you need more information, Moneysmart is a decent starting point as it's independent of the funds. I also like to search '[my super fund] investment options' so I can look at their mixes as well. This is because they give you a general timeframe of how long you should invest in that option to minimise the risk. Here's an overview of some investment types:

- **Growth:** High growth is normally 90% to 100% shares, and it's not recommended by super funds unless the investment will be there for more than five to seven years. That's because if you're due to retire and there is a world event that crashes the share market for a year or more, it's a bad time to pull your money out as it hasn't had time to recover. Regular growth is usually 85% shares.

- **Balanced:** Depending on your fund, your balanced option might be a 50/50 split of shares and cash/fixed interest, 60/40 or 70/30. MySuper (the default option we talked about earlier) is a balanced option. A balanced option is designed to have less drama and more baby llama. The growth years won't be as high, but the low years won't be as low.

- **Cash:** You can choose to have your super in a 'cash investment'. Cash is considered the most conservative option. It does the equivalent of converting your super to the bank deposits we were talking about earlier. It massively reduces the risk of your super balance being affected by downturns and the ups and downs of the stock market. The flipside is that your balance grows very slowly, and usually only in line with inflation.

- **Indexed:** Indexing is the idea of tracking a certain market rather than trying to outperform it. Because it's automated and doesn't have to be managed by people, the fees are usually much lower. If the investment option doesn't have the word 'indexed' in it, that means it is an actively managed option.

- **Ethical:** For some people, it's important to put their money where their mouth is. Most super funds now offer an ethical option. Usually, this is an option that excludes gambling and tobacco, for example. But everyone's ethics are different. Some people are passionate about renewable energy. Some people are passionate about animal rights. Some people are passionate about other industries. It can be difficult to work out if the ethics of the investment align with your own. Ethical funds often have higher fees because the fund managers have to work harder to invest around the ethics of the option.

Getting advice

One of the hardest things about getting advice is the fear of not having a clue what the person is talking about. Well, now you do. Deciding what investment option is best for you might be supremely overwhelming at this point.

It's difficult to recommend advice as it's not affordable for everyone. Super funds offer 'limited personal advice', which is cheaper than a comprehensive plan and can help you understand what might be best for you in terms of investment options.

Limited personal advice is also helpful when a comprehensive service is out of reach and you're looking at consolidating super funds when you have more than one. For example, some of your super funds may have default insurance policies, and some might not.

Rich Aunty Sue action

Log into your super fund and find out what investment option your super balance is currently being invested in. Then, find your fund's fee schedule. This could be in the PDS or another document. Do *not* let them get the better of you. Find it.

Work out your total current fees (investment and performance). Are you happy with this? Also consider the investment option you're in, taking into account the previous definitions. Are you happy with this? Make sure you check all your accounts if you have multiple. If not, it might be time to call your super fund for a chat with their advisors, or find a certified financial planner. You can also keep researching. Your super fund's website will often have some reasonable detail about who each option is suitable for.

Case study: Jo, 52

Jo came to financial counselling as she had sustained an injury, and because she temporarily couldn't work, she needed help with her debts and expenses. Jo wasn't aware that super funds may have an insurance policy for income protection.

Jo looked up her myGov account and had three super funds. Unfortunately, none of them had insurance. Also, Jo wasn't aware she had multiple funds in the first place. As Jo was off work, she spent some time making calls to each fund to understand the fees, charges and investment options so she could decide if consolidating was right for her.

Step 8. Bad performance

How do you know if your super fund has been performing badly? These days, the funds have to tell us. Even better, they have to tell us if they've performed badly for the first year, second year or third year. It's like a school report, and we're the parents who have to sign a letter to say we've seen that our child got a D-minus in chemistry.

Since 2020, APRA has been in charge of testing super performance on our behalf, and it's great. When it comes to testing, they have a benchmark of how funds should be performing and then report on it publicly. In the past, they only reported on MySuper products, but they have started adding some other options, too.

It's important to say that you don't need to change your super fund every year just because it hasn't been the top-performing fund. It's very rare for a super fund to be a top performer for two years in a row, let alone consistently. However, if you're getting letters from your super fund to say it's been a worst performer, maybe it's time to take a look and see why.

Step 9. Insurance*

Under the current legislation, whether you have default insurance in your superannuation depends on your job, super balance and age. So, to check if you have insurance and how much it covers and costs, log in to your super account.

The thing about default insurance is that you get a group insurance policy, which means you don't have to go through health checks like you would with other policies. But, if you cancel it and want to add it later, you generally do. So, I recommend getting advice (through your fund or a third-party advisor) before you cancel it. Your super insurance is normally a low-cover amount and may not be as much as you need, but it's better than nothing. The fees for your insurance are deducted from your super balance.

There are three types of insurance in super:

- **Total and permanent disability (TPD):** This is when you experience some kind of injury or disability that means you won't be able to work again in any job.
- **Life:** This is designed to support your dependants (kids, partner/s etc.) when you die. Your super fund decides who receives this. See the binding death nomination section further on. Note: sometimes TPD and life insurance are linked together and you have to have both or neither.
- **Income protection (IP):** This replaces some of your salary if you can't work due to illness or injury. IP in your super doesn't usually cover job loss, and it's good to be aware of how long you're covered for and for how much. Sometimes it's two years at 75% of your salary, for example.

Insurance is very fiddly, and if you ever make a claim and get turned down, you might want to consider legal advice. Remember, it's in any insurance provider's best financial interests to turn you down if they can.

Rich Aunty Sue action

Log into your super account/s and see what insurance, if any, you have. Are you happy with this? Would it be enough to support your family/modify your home/cover enough of your income? If not, consider seeking advice. Make sure you check all your accounts if you have multiple.

Step 10. Binding death nominations*

Another paragraph, another complicated phrase. It's not you – it's super. A binding death nomination is an easy and important thing in your super that doesn't get explained well enough or often enough. You can request who receives your life/death policy payout in two different ways (I know, so much hot nonsense, who comes up with it?):

- **Non-binding:** In your super account, you can choose who should receive the policy. However, the super fund takes this as more of an 'Okay, babes, we'll think about it' as opposed to actual instructions. They may feel it is more appropriate to give it to someone else, like your kids, even if you've nominated someone else.
- **Binding:** You have to complete a form for this one and can only choose from a certain list – partner, child, other dependant or legal representative. Then you have to get it witnessed by two people who know you. However, this form *is* legally binding (in most instances). A 'lapsing' binding nomination expires after three years while a 'non-lapsing' binding nomination doesn't expire. Everyone should have their binding deathie in place (calling it a deathie makes it sound so much more fun, don't you think?). It takes less than ten minutes. I did mine at work the last few times and had two of my colleagues sign it. Controlling my money from beyond the grave? Hot zombie girl shit.

Rich Aunty Sue action

Get on hot zombie girl shit and *do* your binding death nomination. You can google '[your fund name] binding death form' and that should get you what you need, or go retro by calling your fund and asking for a paper copy to be posted to you.

Step 11. Early release of super

There are very limited circumstances in which you can get your super released early. It makes sense as the money is for your retirement, and what makes it so powerful is its ability to grow over time (remember our examples from Chapter 18).

If you're looking at withdrawing some superannuation early,

I highly recommend that you speak to a financial counsellor first. They will look at all your options and confirm that taking the super out is going to help. Sometimes, taking out super delays the problem rather than solving it.

Grounds for early release of super

There are only a few circumstances in which you are able to withdraw money from your superannuation before your preservation age:

- **Compassionate grounds:** If you need to pay for medical care or funeral expenses, or your home is going to be repossessed by the bank. You apply through the ATO and the lump sum you take out is subject to tax.
- **Terminal illness:** If you have a terminal illness, you can access your super usually within 24 months of your estimated death. You will need to have substantive medical evidence from a couple of different doctors. You apply through your super fund and may be eligible to receive the money tax-free.
- **Severe financial hardship:** If you've been on certain Centrelink payments for more than six months and need funds for essential living expenses. Your super fund makes the assessment. Again, seeing a financial counsellor first can be a great help, especially if you have debts as part of these expenses.

There are other reasons, such as permanent and temporary incapacity, which link in with the insurances we talked about earlier. Taking out your super early should always be a last resort, and a financial counsellor will look at other options with you, including those you might not have known about.

Step 12. How it all comes together

Yes, your retirement is quite possibly a good few years away. But think about how quickly the last year has gone, or the last five years. Time races away from us as we get older, but time is power when it comes to your superannuation. The ultimate goal is to stand on the edge of retirement and do a trust fall into rich Aunty Sue's arms. Don't break a hip.

Here are some short and sharp points on retirement when it comes to your super:

- Except in extreme circumstances, you can't withdraw your super until you reach preservation age (beef jerky age) and have retired. For most of us, that's 60.
- If you are still working at 60, you can 'transition to retirement', which is a set-up that lets you access some super while you're winding down. Your financial advisor or super fund can help you with this strategy. If you're using Centrelink, you can speak to the Financial Information Service, which is a free government service.
- Even if you're still working, you can access your super at 65.

Some people want to (or do) retire before their preservation age. Remember, any money you add to your super during your early working years gets locked away, so make sure you won't need that money sooner. Note: First Home Super Saver Scheme is exempt from this rule.

Rich Aunty Sue action

Consider speaking to an advisor, either through your fund or privately, as you get close to retirement age. Make sure you have structured your withdrawals and cash flow as effectively as possible.

Waffle cone gelato

(takeaways) from Chapter 21

Decide your schedule for working through the steps. You might want to do one step a week, or two steps every weekend.

_____

Once you've decided, diarise your sessions.

_____

Keep notes on what you're doing and learning and save them so you can refer to them during the process. They'll also help when you come back to them down the track for reviewing purposes.

 ## Reflective questions

Aunty Sue's 12-step program has given you plenty to work through, so we won't add any extra questions for this chapter.

Conclusion

Last bits and bobs

We've come full circle – we've done it. What a monster Part 3 was, and yet here we are, on the cusp of finishing the book. I hope you're feeling empowered, engaged and ready to work with your money for the rest of your life.

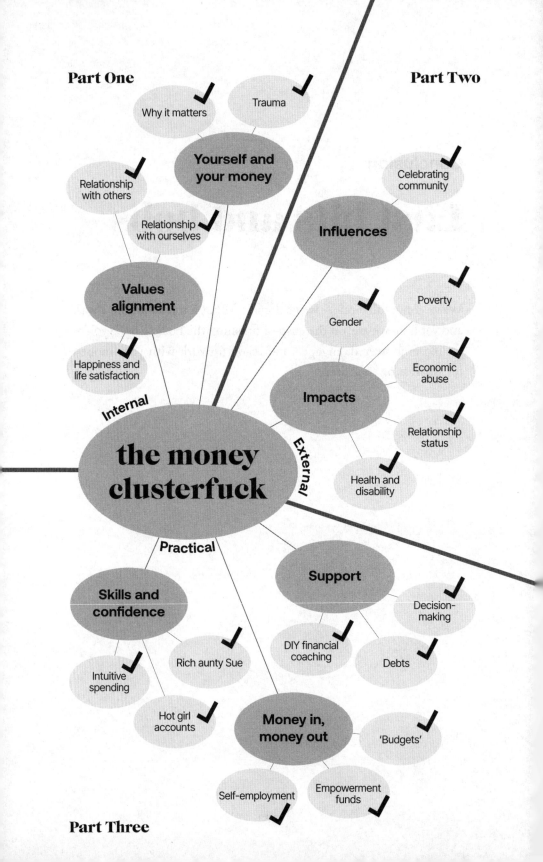

Part One

Part Two

the money
clusterfuck

Internal

External

Practical

**Yourself and
your money**

Why it matters

Trauma

Relationship
with others

Relationship
with ourselves

**Values
alignment**

Happiness and
life satisfaction

Influences

Celebrating
community

Gender

Poverty

Impacts

Economic
abuse

Relationship
status

Health and
disability

Support

Decision-
making

DIY financial
coaching

Debts

**Skills and
confidence**

Rich aunty Sue

Intuitive
spending

Hot girl
accounts

**Money in,
money out**

'Budgets'

Self-employment

Empowerment
funds

Part Three

What happens next is up to you. You may have worked through the practical steps as you read, or you may be planning to go back now and work through them step by step. You can also lean into any of the reflective questions at the end of the chapters.

Remember our fail-fast method from Chapter 16? It's okay to try something and for it to not work quite as you intended. As you test your new systems, focus on keeping the good and tweaking the less good. It's perfectly fine to go through the chapters slowly, or re-read them now and in the future. Normal money, not perfect money.

Whatever you do, if it's an improvement on whatever system you had running before, that is worth celebrating. If life gets in the way and you find yourself on a break from doing the work – either practical or emotional – these parts, frameworks, concepts, cauldrons and matrices will be here to pick you back up. In the meantime, I hope you fall in love with learning about yourself and your money.

It's important to remember that you don't have to take every single point on board. Hell, I've read money books and not understood everything they talked about.

When you know yourself, *really* know yourself, and what's important to you, you can start exploring money books without implementing every tip. There are some recommended books in the next section. Start wherever you like.

You can also choose where you want to take the journey next. Do you want to jump into other money books, work on privilege or something else we talked about? Either way, it's been a pleasure walking this journey with you. The train has left the station and it's headed in the direction of your choosing.

LOVEYOUBYE.

Further reading

There will be chapters and themes that resonated with you more than others. I've included further reading resources, both for money and non-money parts, so you can explore whatever areas interest you.

Money: general skills and concepts

- *The Richest Man in Babylon* – George S Clason
- *How Much is Enough? Making Financial Decisions that Create Wealth and Well-being* – Arun Abey and Andrew Ford
- *Your Money or Your Life* – Joe Dominguez and Vicki Robin
- *Die With Zero* – Bill Perkins
- *Good With Money* – Emma Edwards
- *Financial Feminist* – Tori Dunlap
- *How to be a Super Smart Woman* – Pauline Taylor
- *Money School* – Lacey Filipich
- *Kids Ain't Cheap* – Ana Kresina
- *Buying Happiness* – Kate Campbell
- *The Millionaire Next Door* – Thomas J. Stanley and William D. Danko
- *The Psychology of Money* – Morgan Housel
- *Superannuation Made Simple* – Noel Whittaker
- *The Barefoot Investor* – Scott Pape
- *I Will Teach You to be Rich* – Ramit Sethi
- *Money with Jess* – Jessica Irvine

Money: investing and growing wealth

- *Girls that Invest* – Simran Kaur
- *Strong Money Australia* – Dave Gow
- *How to Not Work Forever* – Natasha Etschmann and Ana Kresina
- *The Little Book of Common-Sense Investing* – John C. Bogle
- *The 4-Hour Work Week* – Timothy Ferriss
- *Rich Dad Poor Dad* – Robert T. Kiyosaki

Life and relationships

- *Four Thousand Weeks* – Oliver Burkeman
- *The Circles* – Kerry Armstrong
- *The Joy of Being Selfish* – Michelle Elman
- *Setting Boundaries* – Dr Rebecca Ray
- *Attached:* – Amir Levine and Rachel Heller
- *I Don't* – Clementine Ford
- *Going Solo* – Eric Klinenberg
- *All the Single Ladies* – Rebecca Traister

Poverty

- *Scarcity: Why Having Too Little Means So Much* – Sendhil Mullainathan and Eldar Shafir
- *Bridges out of Poverty: Strategies for Professionals and Communities* – Philip E. DeVol, Ruby K Payne and Terie Dreussi Smith

Privilege, race and intersectionality

- *Demarginalizing the Intersection of Race and Sex* – Kimberlé Crenshaw
- *The Urgency of Intersectionality | TED Talk* – Kimberlé Crenshaw
- *Dark Emu* – Bruce Pascoe
- *Growing up Disabled in Australia* – Carly Findlay
- *Growing up African in Australia* – Maxine Beneba Clarke
- *Too Migrant, Too Muslim, Too Loud* – Mehreen Faruqi
- *White Fragility* – Robin DiAngelo

- *Finding the Heart of the Nation: The Journey of the Uluru Statement towards Voice, Treaty and Truth* – Thomas Mayo
- *Welcome to Country* – Marcia Langton
- *Unorthodox: The Scandalous Rejection of My Hasidic Roots* – Deborah Feldman
- *White Rage: The Unspoken Truth of Our Racial Divide* – Carol Anderson
- *Educated* – Tara Westover
- *I Am Malala: The Story of the Girl Who Stood Up for Education and Was Shot by the Taliban* – Malala Yousafzai
- *Why I'm No Longer Talking to White People About Race* – Reni Eddo-Lodge
- *Talkin' Up to the White Woman: Indigenous Women and Feminism* – Aileen Moreton-Robinson
- *So You Want to Talk About Race* – Ijeoma Oluo

Economic abuse

- *See What You Made Me Do* – Jess Hill
- *Domestic Economic Abuse* – Supriya Singh

Disordered eating and body image

- *Just Eat It: How Intuitive Eating Can Help You Get Your Shit Together Around Food* – Laura Thomas
- *Secrets of Feeding a Healthy Family* – Ellyn Satter
- *Intuitive Eating, 4th Edition* – Evelyn Tribole and Elyse Resch
- *The Beauty Myth* – Naomi Wolf
- *Body Positive Power* – Megan Jayne Crabbe
- *Beauty Sick* – Renee Engeln
- *The Body is Not an Apology* – Sonya Renee Taylor
- *Body of Truth* – Harriet Brown

Glossary

AAT
Administrative Appeals Tribunal. AAT has the power to review certain decisions made by the federal departments and agencies. It will reassess a decision made by legislation to see if that was the correct outcome.

ABN
Australian Business Number – an individual number held by sole traders, partnerships, and companies to identify them as being or operating a business.

AFCA
Australian Financial Complaints Authority. An independent and impartial non-profit that reviews complaints about financial services for customers, which the financial institution has to follow if AFCA decides it has done something wrong.

APRA
Australian Prudential Regulation Authority. An independent federal body in charge of making sure financial services are stable and competitive.

Binding death benefit nomination
A specific way of letting your superannuation fund know that you have clear intentions on who should get your super balance when you die. Requires a witnessed form, and normally needs to be renewed every three years.

BNPL	Buy now pay later. Financial products that are offered as no interest and with split payment instalments. While they do not charge interest, they do charge fees such as late fees. Afterpay, humm, Zip Pay are all examples of BNPL providers.
Centrelink	Australia's social security program which is managed by Services Australia. There is a range of payments to support people who need extra support. Payments include:
	JobSeeker: for people currently unemployed, to support them while they look for work.
	Parenting Payment: for people who are a young child's primary carer.
	Disability Support Pension: for people who have a condition or disability that will affect them for more than two years and stops them from working.
Concessional contributions	Extra money put into your superannuation by you, separately to the mandatory amount by your employer. Concessional contributions are done by salary sacrifice, before tax, and are generally processed by your payroll officer. Non-concessional contributions/voluntary contributions are made after tax, directly by you.
Conscious bias	Where you knowingly take actions, make decisions or make assumptions about a person or group of people that you wouldn't make about other people.
Cultural competence	Historically it was used in healthcare and is a person's ability to understand and support people from different social and cultural backgrounds, generally when supporting patients. It's used more broadly in areas such as community services and businesses now.

Cultural safety	Looks beyond individuals to the systems and power imbalances that can affect a person's outcomes. It focuses on equity of outcomes between people of different backgrounds, rather than focusing on connecting with and supporting one person.
Customer Advocate	An independent person or team within a bank that helps the bank better understand what customers and communities need. Customer Advocates bring the customer voice within the bank, and help the bank to sustain a culture of responsible and fair banking.
Diet culture	A social perception that thinness equals health, and that foods are split into 'good' and 'bad'. The idea that a person's body size can determine if they are 'healthy' or 'unhealthy'. Diet culture is based on ever-changing myths about different foods and habits, which means no one can ever quite succeed at it.
Dole bludger	An offensive slang term that is generally used to imply a person is on Centrelink because they 'don't want' to find a job.
Domestic/family violence	A pattern of behaviour and/or control against another person which is a violation or 'violence' against their human rights. The behaviour is used to create a power imbalance to cause harm. It can include financial, economic, emotional, technological, sexual, physical and religious abuse, as well as coercive control and stalking.
Economic abuse	Deliberate, strategic use of power to deprive another person of resources, autonomy and dignity. It is broader than financial abuse, and extends to a person's freedom and ability to get a job, have social connections and support their children.

Emergency fund/ empowerment fund	Money set aside to support a person in a financial emergency, or when they need to remove themselves from a particular situation and need money to do so.
Experience dividends	A term used by Bill Perkins to refer to the 'dividends' or later happiness a person can get from a positive experience or memory from earlier in their life.
FEE-HELP	Government loan for university or other higher education providers to cover fees that then gets paid back when a person reaches a certain income level. FEE-HELP is for students who don't have a place supported by the Commonwealth under HECS-HELP.
Financial abuse	Where a person exerts control and power by withholding money, controlling all the family finances and/or making the other person sign for loans or other debts. The control is used to harm the other person and violate their human rights.
Financial advisor/ financial planner	A qualified professional who works with you to understand and plan for your short, medium and long-term goals. A financial advisor can help with financial matters including cashflow and preparing for life events such as retirement.
Financial coach	A person who works to help people understand their financial and other strengths, triggers and behaviours, and develop financial resilience and confidence. A person does not have to be qualified to be a financial coach.
Financial counsellor	A professional who helps people through advice and advocacy when they are in financial difficulty. Most financial counsellors are qualified, though there are some who are qualified by experience rather than formal education.

Financial hardship/financial difficulty	Where a person is struggling or unable to make ends meet for their bills, debts and general living costs.
Financial Information Service	A government service for people on Centrelink payments. Usually used as a person is getting older. FIS can provide information on financial aspects, including on investments, salary sacrificing and credit.
Financial integrity	Having awareness, empathy and patience for the way external factors influence both practical and behavioural money experiences.
Financial literacy	The ability to understand concepts and skills relating to money and finance, and put them into practice in a safe way.
Financial privilege	Accessibility to resources that create better opportunities for financial stability and wealth.
Generational poverty	A family that has lived in poverty for at least two generations.
Generational wealth	Money, and/or assets that have been passed down or inherited from one generation to another.
HECS-HELP	A government loan to help you pay study fees at university or an approved higher education provider. HECS-HELP is for students who have a Commonwealth Supported Place (CSP), which is where the government subsidises part of a person's studies.
Inflation	How much more goods and services increase in cost over a certain amount of time, which is usually measured yearly.

Intersectionality	Historically used to reference the particular intersection of discrimination Black women experience through a combination of racism and sexism. Now colloquially used to refer to different types of personal and social factors that intersect with each other and have an impact on how a person moves through the world and the opportunities that are available to them.
Intuitive eating	Eating in a way that reflects a person's hunger and fullness, as well as desires. A method designed to support people returning to 'normal eating'.
IUI	Intrauterine insemination, a fertility treatment where specially prepared sperm is put directly in a person's uterus.
IVF	In vitro fertilisation, a fertility treatment where mature eggs are taken from a person's ovaries and fertilised manually by sperm in a lab which becomes an embryo. One or more of the fertilised eggs is placed in the person's uterus.
Matrices	More than one matrix.
Mortgage	A loan used to buy a home, that is paid back with interest.
National Debt Helpline	An independent, confidential service where you can speak to a financial counsellor on the phone or by webchat for free.
NDIS/NDIA	The NDIS (National Disability Insurance Scheme) is administered by the NDIA (National Disability Insurance Agency) which is an independent statutory agency. The NDIS provides funding to people with disability to improve their quality of life, access to support and participation in the community.
Non-monogamous	A relationship or relationship style that involves more than two people. Non-monogamous relationships can work in many ways.

Personal loan	A loan taken out for a specific purpose that is repaid over a fixed number of years. There are two types of personal loans. A secured personal loan is when you get a personal loan for an item such as a car or boat. The loan will often be at a lower interest rate, but they reserve the right to take back the item if you stop making the payments. An unsecured loan is when there is no item for the loan, and it usually has a higher interest rate.
Preservation age	The minimum age a person has to reach before they can access their superannuation.
Salary sacrificing	Where an employee gives up some of their pre-tax salary and this money is paid by the employer to something else such as superannuation, a car or shares.
Savings account	A bank account where you deposit money and generally earn interest on that money. A savings account usually does not come with a debit card.
Sinking funds	Bank accounts that a person sets up for a specific purpose – and then sinks money into those accounts for that purpose.
Situational poverty	Poverty that occurs as a result of a life event or series of life events. It might be short-term, such as a job loss, a death in the family or a temporary injury. It could be an unaffordable increase to the cost of living, or a permanent injury that changes a person's ability to work.
Situationship	Generally the same as 'friends with benefits'. Some kind of relationship where you aren't committed, but are more than friends – often sexual partners.
Social security	See Centrelink.

Sole trader	A self-employed person who runs their own business. The income from a sole trader business gets added to a person's total personal income and tax is paid at the individual's tax rate.
Statement of financial position	A document that outlines someone's income, assets, expenses and debts. It is often used by creditors to understand a person's situation before offering financial hardship assistance.
Superannuation	Money that gets put aside for retirement. It is a compulsory payment by employers from total wages.
Tax	A charge that has to be paid. Income tax in Australia refers to money taken out of wages, business income or other earnings and is used to support public services such as social security, education and defence.
Throuple	A consensual relationship between three people where the three people are romantically connected to each other.
Transaction account	A bank account that is usually for day-to-day banking and often has a debit card to make purchases.
Unconscious bias	Taking action, making decisions or making assumptions about a person or group of people that you wouldn't make for or about other people, without realising it is occurring.
Voluntary superannuation contributions	Extra money put into your superannuation by you, separately to the mandatory amount by your employer. Non-concessional contributions are made after tax, directly by you.

Acknowledgements

In homage to *Sister Act 2*, these acknowledgements are spirited and longwinded.

Know Your Worth was written on the lands of the oldest story-tellers of all time. It was written on Noongar boodja, land of the Whadjuk people; and on the land of the Gadigal people of the Eora nation. Always was, always will be Aboriginal land.

Firstly, thank you to our storytellers. I have read each of your contributions more than 100 times during this process, and every time I have the same feeling of awe for your honesty, passion and vulnerability. Jude, Bonnie, 'Renee', Craig, 'Joan', 'Max', 'Ashley', Tobiasz, Mastura, 'Ada A', and Madonna, thank you. The book is better for having your voices in it.

My absolute huge bloody thanks also:

To my Zeida, Phil, who has held me in unwavering high regard all my life, and has been proud about anything and everything I have ever told him, from making a curry to writing a book.

To my mum, Julie (aka 'Motherrrrr'), who has seen me at my absolute best highs and absolute worst lows over the last 24 months (well, life), and did an entire proofread for me. To my brother Lachlan, for the steady stream of LOTR content. To my cousin Cameron, for bringing me bread, packed lunchboxes and 1/2 of my favourite small children, Ladybug.

A great work leader is a rare find, and I have had two in a row. Richard Usher has been my champion since day bubbles. There would have been no bad.bitch.money without bbrichardisms. Thank you for letting me play to my strengths and do so many things that mattered. I simply wouldn't be where I am without you. thumbs up emoji. Ben Griffin, whose passion, determination and generosity is second only to the way he somehow knows enough on every single topic I ask him about to help me. Thank you for trusting without hesitation that I could hold down a full-time job, study a law degree and write a book all at the same time.

To the Affirm Press team, for bringing *Know Your Worth* to life. Special thanks to Kelly Doust, for her wisdom, warmth and genuine love for making books their best, and to Laura Franks (Frank-Kay), for her exquisite project management and good-natured tolerance of my unhinged editing behaviour. Thank you to Gabriella Sterio, for her kind words and flawless copyedit, and to Alissa Dinallo for the cover design of the decade.

The 8th wonder in this world is the way women support each other.

Thank you to Emma Edwards, the Paddington to my Pippin, who hiked this journey first and showed me where to tread. To Lacey Filipich, whose sage advice was one of the key pieces that got me to this exact moment, and has said my name in a room of opportunities many times. To the group chats: The Charmed Ones – Steph and Hannah; Chaos Corner – Jess and Bianca; The Finance Witches – Deline and Helen; Troy's Angels (including JE Bosley); the Cliterati – Carly, Kiri, Alison and Sarah; and '9 December' chat – Madoona, Kate, TP and badbitchgrandma, thank you, thank you, thank you. To Jess N, who had unshakable confidence in my ability to get this off the ground from the beginning.

To Em Fed-woods, for her ability to listen, her constant thoughtful support and for bringing me the other 1/2 of my favourite small humans, Stelly Watermelly. Thank you for convincing me to keep going in 2018 when I was full-body sobbing over how hard I was working and getting nowhere, and for sticking with me while I then worked twice as hard for three times as long.

To my dearest Dani, who has wholeheartedly supported me, despite the fact I have worked on something during every holiday we've ever taken and cried about it. You were there on that most special camel ride in 2021, where I realised a new story arc had started, and have been a key character in the plot from the pilot episode. Sorry about the time I called you in the middle of the night in California to tell you I'd signed to write a book and you thought someone had died.

To Ashton, for the CrossFit Saturdays that were sometimes the only exercise I did that week, and the coffee dates that always went much longer than they should have but were never long enough.

Additional thanks:

To my early readers, Jenny and Chris, Cameron, and Shannon, and my subject matter experts, Madonna, Deline and Bianca. Very big thanks to Ellyn Sattler for her genuine interest in my 'normal money' take on her 'normal eating', and for allowing me to reference her work in full.

To my fellow law student colleagues – especially Michael Bamford and Hugh Marshall, who helped me through the trimesters leading up to and during this book. You were the difference between making it and not. Extra love especially to Stephanie Paige Hupfeld, P Huppy, the salt to my vinegar. I could not have done it without you bestie, oh my fucking boots, simply no.

To Janine Parker, for the original bbm branding and marketing advice and supporting it from day dot. To Dervy Parker, for the burgers. To James McHale, for 'mad witch honey'. To Matt, for the webdev and helping me vacuum behind my oven that time.

Thank you, finally, to anyone I have accidentally missed. Here is a space for your name in case we need to write it in manually

_____.

LOVEYOUBYE.